MEET THE AUTHOR

Paul Mayer has authored four nationally best-selling cookbooks. For many years, he travelled throughout the world and wrote commentary on food, restaurants and hotels. Presently he lives in San Francisco and owns and operates a food catering business.

THIS QUICHE AND SOUFFLE COOKBOOK MAKES FRENCH COOKING EASY

- Authored by San Francisco's renowned Paul Mayer.

- Covers everything you ever wanted to know about quiche making—what kinds of pans to use plus a wide variety of pastry and custards to use in their preparation.

- Includes a detailed step-by-step guide to making souffles that rise every time. Whether your passion is a chocolate souffle or a simple cheese souffle, you will find it within these pages.

- For easy use, this book lies flat when opened, contains one recipe per page, is printed in large, easy-to-read type and takes a minimum of counter space.

SATISFACTION GUARANTEE — If you are not completely satisfied with this book, your purchase price will gladly be refunded. Simply return it to us within 30 days along with your receipt.

Quiche

by Paul Mayer

Illustrated by MIKE NELSON

A Nitty Gritty Book*
Published by
Nitty Gritty Productions
P. O. Box 5457
Concord, California 94524

*Nitty Gritty Books - Trademark
Owned by Nitty Gritty Productions
Concord, California

ISBN 0-911954-72-4
Library of Congress Catalog Card Number: 77-670105

16th Printing

TABLE OF CONTENTS

A TART APART

That the Quiche is not even French seems a very distinct probability! Etymology is often at best selective, but it looks very much as if the word "quiche," which in French refers only to the specific custard-filled tart, could have, in fact, derived from the German. To arrive at this conclusion it is only necessary to remember these facts:

a) The Quiche is indigenous to the regions of Alsace and Lorraine—particularly the latter. Both of these areas, although part of France today, have in the past been part of Germany. Indeed, they have been political footballs more than once. With roads in France what they are today, it is often easier to reach these borderline areas by using the German autobahns than it is to battle one's way across the minimal highways of eastern France. Furthermore, although French is, of course, the official language of the region, the people are equally at home with German. Towns and cities have frankly German names, or Frenchified versions of them. For example: Metz, or Strasbourg, or Illheusern and Ammerschwihr, to mention only a few.

b) The German word for "kitchen" is *Küche*.

c) The ǘ sound in German is a very tight one, more like the hard "i" as in the English word "quick."
d) The word "Quiche" is sometimes spelled "Kiche."
e) The French "Qu" is never pronounced any other way except as a hard sound like the letter "K"—a letter which appears very infrequently in the French language.

2   Therefore, it seems quite likely that early travelers to Lorraine, having enjoyed this savory tart baked with custard around and over cheese, took the dish with them to other parts of France. Whereas in Lorraine itself the dish was probably untitled, it began appearing in other menus elsewhere as "Une Specialite de la Kǘche Lorraine," and from there the transition from *kǘche* to "*kiche*" to the more common phonetic spelling of *Quiche* was but a matter of time. As the dish became better known it was no longer necessary to remind diners that this was a specialty of the Lorraine kitchen, and so the lengthy phrase was shortened to its present day form.

Since its early days, the term "quiche," in a strict sense, has referred only to one custard tart—filled with cheese, or perhaps bacon and cheese, or ham and cheese, covered with custard, baked, and served—usually free-standing, but sometimes in the pretty dish in which it was cooked. Lately, however, there has been a growing tendency to call any pie shell, filled with any savory mixture, be it meats, seafood, or vegetable, and similarly filled with custard before baking—a quiche, although actually they should be called flans.

Indeed, the metal rings in which the pie shells are formed for Quiche Lorraine and other of these dishes are known as flan rings. But it does seem eminently sensible, to this author at any rate, to end the confusion and dichotomy of terms and bunch the whole business under the one all-encompassing word.

You will find that the quiche is a most versatile and agreeable fellow! It is at home almost everywhere, in every type of dish, and for every occasion. It can function as an hors d'oeuvre, a luncheon entree, a vegetable, on the brunch or buffet table. In much the same manner as an omelette, it can be filled with just about anything, which makes it an excellent way to use up small amounts of leftovers. And to top it all off—a boon to today's servantless hostess—its components may be prepared well ahead of time, and the filled shell simply covered with the already beaten custard and popped into the oven when party time approaches.

Here, then, is a "Collection of Quiches"—some of every type—to enhance your table, and—at the same time—your reputation as a cook.

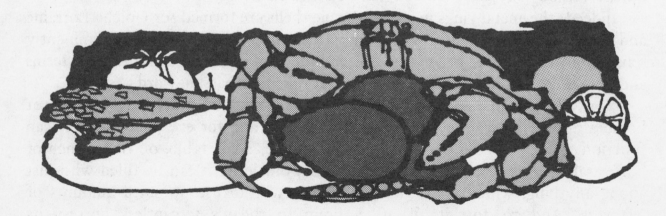

RINGS AND THINGS

The original quiche was, no doubt, baked in a pottery plate, but as time went on, it became customary to serve quiches free-standing and so the flan ring was developed. Since it is merely a metal hoop, it must always rest on a cookie sheet or spring-form bottom.

The flan ring—refined—is a pie tin with a removable bottom, now more commonly called a quiche pan. Quiche pans come in many sizes and usually have fluted sides. They are highly recommended since quiches baked in fluted pans and brought to the table free-standing on a plate are always an impressive sight. A quiche pan with a removable bottom makes this trick easy!

If you prefer, there are many beautiful porcelain quiche dishes available in all sizes. Quiches baked in porcelain dishes are never served free-standing but must go to the table in the dish in which they were baked.

But, please, don't put off trying these recipes simply because you lack the appropriate dish. If it's not more than 1-1/4 inches deep, an ordinary layer-cake tin or pie plate will do admirably if that's all you happen to have. Then, when you have the opportunity, look around! You will find quiche receptacles galore. The recipes given here can be used with a variety of pans and rings, such as: Flan rings—8" x 1-1/4"—Quiche pans—8" x 1-1/4" or 9" x 7/8"—Porcelain dishes—8" x 1-1/4". If a pan happens to be larger, the quiche will be thinner. If smaller, there will be custard left over. All the following recipes may be successfully doubled, or tripled to fit other and larger sizes.

THREE PASTRIES — OR IS IT FOUR!

CLASSIC QUICHE PASTRY—Use with quiche pan, flan ring or porcelain dish.

1 cup + 2 tbs. flour	3 tbs. firm butter	2-5 tbs. ice cold milk
pinch salt	3 tbs. vegetable shortening	

Sift flour and salt into bowl. Using fingers or a pastry blender, cut butter and shortening into flour. Work quickly and lightly. Rub flour and fat through fingertips until mixture is fine and mealy. Start mixing the dough gently as you add cold milk, 1 tablespoon at a time. Add milk until mixture just gathers into a firm, yet crumbly ball. Do not exert any pressure to force the dough together. The less milk you can use, the flakier the pastry will be. Roll dough between 2 sheets of waxed paper. Line pan, being careful not to stretch pastry. Prick all over inner surfaces, including sides, with tines of fork. Paint surface with a very small amount of unbeaten egg white. Partially bake shell on lowest rack of 450°F. oven 8 to 12 minutes or until lightly browned and set. Check shell after 5 minutes and gently push down puffy spots. Repeat if neccessary. Cool partially baked crust 10 minutes, then fill and bake as directed in the quiche recipe of your choice.

RICH QUICHE PASTRY—Use with quiche pan, flan ring or porcelain dish.

1-1/2 cups flour
1/4 cup butter
4 egg yolks

1/4 cup grated Parmesan cheese
pinch salt, cayenne, dry mustard
1-3 tbs. ice cold milk

Place flour in bowl. Make a well in center of flour. Put butter, egg yolks, cheese, salt, cayenne and dry mustard in well. With fingers of one hand, work all center ingredients into a smooth paste. Quickly work in flour. Add only enough ice cold milk, 1 tablespoon at a time, to make the dough gather. Shape into a smooth ball. Roll out on floured surface. Line pan, being careful not to stretch pastry. Prick all over inner surfaces, including sides, with tines of fork. Paint surface with very small amount of unbeaten egg white. Partially bake shell on lowest rack of 450°F. oven 8 to 12 minutes or until lightly browned and set. Check shell after 5 minutes and gently push down puffy spots. Repeat if necessary. Cool partially baked crust about 10 minutes, then fill and bake as directed in the quiche recipe of your choice.

CHEESIE QUICHE PASTRY—Do not use this crust with a flan ring.

3/4 cup flour
1/4 lb. butter
2 oz. Velveeta cheese

10   Place flour, butter and Velveeta cheese in bowl. (And at last, something justifies the existence of Velveeta.) Work these ingredients together until they gather into a ball. If dough is too soft to handle, chill for 10 minutes. Roll out on a heavily floured surface. Line pan being careful not to stretch pastry. Prick all over inner surfaces, including sides, with tines of fork. Partially bake shell on lowest rack of 450°F. oven about 8 minutes or until lightly browned and set. Check shell after 5 minutes and gently push down puffy spots. Repeat if necessary. Cool partially baked crust about 10 minutes, then fill and bake as directed in the quiche recipe of your choice.

QUICK AND EASY QUICHE PASTRY—A very acceptable puff pastry shell can be made this way.

1 package Pepperidge Farm Frozen Patty Shells

Completely thaw 6 patty shells. Press together well. Roll out on lightly floured surface. Fit into pan. Prick bottom and sides well with tines of fork. Paint with small amount of unbeaten egg white. Fill and bake as directed in the quiche recipe of your choice.

Except for pastries rolled out between two sheets of waxed paper, I always transfer the dough to the pan by rolling it up onto the rolling pin. Lift it over the dish and carefully unroll it again. When the dough has been rolled between paper, I lift away the top paper. Then invert the dough, still on the paper, and place it over the dish. Before pressing it into the dish, I remove the remaining paper so there are no wrinkles in the dough to catch the paper and rip the dough.

TWO CUSTARDS

CUSTARD A — slightly richer and firmer
1 cup whipping cream   pinch salt, cayenne, nutmeg
4 egg yolks

   Blend ingredients together. Use as directed in the quiche recipe of your choice, pages 14 thru 85.

CUSTARD B — uses whole egg plus extra yolks
1/2 cup whipping cream   1 whole egg + 2 egg yolks
1/2 cup half and half   pinch salt, cayenne, nutmeg

   Blend ingredients together. Use as directed in the quiche recipe of your choice, pages 14 thru 85.

   Armed with pastries and custards, you are now ready to make the quiche of your choice. So let's begin with Quiche Lorraine, the Granddaddy of them all. It makes 4 to 6 servings as do all recipes in this book.

QUICHE LORRAINE

Quiche pastry   6 to 8 slices bacon
Custard   8 ozs. Gruyere cheese

Fry bacon until very crisp. Drain on paper towels. Slice cheese. Fill prepared quiche shell with overlapping slices of cheese and bacon. Pour on custard. Bake in preheated 375°F. oven 35-45 minutes, or until custard is puffed and tests completely done and pastry is nicely browned. Allow to rest 5 minutes before serving. Note: Sometimes in France, blanched salt pork cut into julienne strips is substituted for the smokier tasting bacon.

14

QUICHE LORRAINE II

Follow recipe for Quiche Lorraine, but fill shell with tiny cubes of ham and Gruyere cheese. Pour on custard. Bake as directed.

Pastry recipes on pages 8-11   Custards on page 13

CAN I SUBSTITUTE? PLEASE DO!

In a world where we are bombarded continually with prohibitions—"No Smoking"—"No Parking"—"No Left Turn"—"No Talking To The Operator While The Bus Is In Motion"—it appears to me that one of the most damnable of all the "no's" is that one at the bottom of so many menus—"No Substitutions"! After all, pleasing one's palate is a personal matter and the choice should be ours. Some of your favorite recipes are probably those you or your mother adapted by substituting ingredients which the family likes best. Substituting allows us to give vent to our creative desires. And, looking at it from strickly a practical standpoint, it enables us to use a recipe that calls for an item we don't happen to have on hands, by simply substituting something we do have and, perhaps, like better anyway! I wonder, if substitution and not necessity was the mother of invention. So here, then, are some variations on QUICHE LORRAINE—just a few—but the range is endless if you will give your imagination free rein.

QUICHE LORRAINE VARIATIONS
WITH CHEDDAR OR MUNSTER

Follow recipe for Quiche Lorraine. Substitute slices of well aged Cheddar or domestic Munster for Gruyere. Bake as directed.

WITH PARMESAN

Follow recipe for Quiche Lorraine. Use freshly grated Parmesan cheese instead of Gruyere. Place layer of crisp bacon in bottom of shell. Sprinkle on 1/2 cup Parmesan. Repeat layers until shell is filled. Pour on custard. Bake in preheated 375°F. oven 40-50 minutes, or until custard is puffed and tests completely done and pastry is nicely browned. Allow to rest 3-4 minutes before serving.

QUICHES WITH VEGETABLES

Since the quiche, other than "a la Lorraine," lends itself to almost any part of the meal, it seems quite natural for it to assume the role of both starch and vegetable together. Actually, the richness of the custard and the brightness of variegated vegetable both serve to enhance the more simply prepared meats, such as roasts or grills. The kinds of vegetable used are limited only to your imagination and, of course, other things may be added to the greens as well. Here are just a few of the many, many combinations which you can use.

THE PAUL MAYER METHOD FOR COOKING GREEN VEGETABLES

This method yields brilliant, tasty peas, beans, brussels sprouts, asparagus and broccoli. Don't ask me why it works, but it does! I think it's because the water is never allowed to stop boiling all the time the vegetables are cooking.

Bring a tea kettle full of water to a rapid boil, and KEEP IT BOILING!!!!!!! In another pot, which can be fitted with a lid, place a large handful of sugar and 1 teaspoon salt. Place this second pot over high heat. Heat the pot until the sugar melts and just begins to caramelize. Then place the washed and trimmed vegetables (Remember! Green ones only!) in the pot. With the heat still at its highest point, pour over the boiling water from the tea kettle. Clap the lid on the pot, and boil furiously for 7 minutes—not 8, or 6, or 5-1/2, or 9—but 7 minutes—before draining off the boiling water. Rinse briefly in cold water to stop the cooking. The vegetables WILL stay hot! Season with salt, pepper and a little melted butter, or use as indicated in the recipe. Please bear in mind that this method does NOT apply to root vegetables, eggplant, artichokes or spinach.

ARTICHOKE & DILL PICKLE QUICHE

Quiche pastry
Custard
12 small artichokes
2 tbs. tarragon vinegar
1 tsp. salt

3-4 whole peppercorns
bay leaf
salt, pepper
2-3 tbs. butter
1 finely chopped Kosher-style dill

20   Trim leaves from artichokes so that only the edible part of the heart remains. Cover with boiling water. Add vinegar, salt, peppercorns and bay leaf. Cook 10 minutes or until tender. Drain well. Shake in pot over heat to drive off any excess moisture. Add butter and toss until hearts are well coated. Season with salt and pepper. Place in prepared quiche shell. Sprinkle with dill pickle. Pour custard over all. Bake in preheated 375°F. oven 35-45 minutes, or until custard has set, is deep brown and tests done when knife comes clean from center of quiche. Allow to stand 2-3 minutes before serving.

Pastry recipes on pages 8-11 Custards on page 13

FRESH ASPARAGUS QUICHE

Quiche pastry
Custard
1-1/2 lbs. fresh asparagus
1 cup freshly grated Parmesan cheese

Discard tough part of asparagus. Wash spears thoroughly. Cut into 1-inch pieces. Cook according to method given on page 19. Drain thoroughly. Toss with Parmesan until well coated. Place in prepared quiche shell. Pour custard over all. Bake in preheated 375°F. oven 35-40 minutes, or until custard is set and pastry is nicely browned. Allow to stand 3-4 minutes before serving.

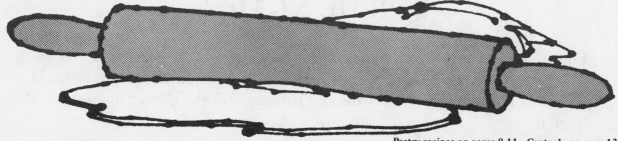

Pastry recipes on pages 8-11   Custards on page 13

GREEN BEAN & ALMOND QUICHE

Quiche pastry   1/2 lb. fresh green beans   2 oz. slivered almonds
Custard   2 tbs. butter

Wash and string beans. Cook according to the method given on page 19. Drain thoroughly. Cut into small pieces, crosswise. Melt butter. Add almonds. Cook gently until they begin to color. Add beans. Cook 2-3 minutes. Place in prepared quiche shell. Pour custard over all. Bake in preheated 375°F. oven 40-45 minutes, or until custard is set, tests done and pastry is nicely browned.

22

QUICHE NICOISE

Follow recipe for Green Bean Quiche. Omit almonds. Peel, seed and chop 1 large tomato. Cook in 3 tablespoons butter until reduced and dry. Mash 1/2 can anchovies to a paste. Mix with beans and tomato. Fill shell. Pour on custard. Bake as directed.

Pastry recipes on pages 8-11   Custards on page 13

BRUSSELS SPROUTS & CHESTNUT QUICHE

Quiche pastry
Custard
1/2 lb. Brussels sprouts
1 tbs. butter
1/2 lb. chestnuts
2 tbs. butter
peanut oil

Wash and trim Brussels sprouts. Cook according to method given on page 19. Toss with 1 tablespoon butter. Make a criss-cross slit on flat side of chestnuts. Heat 2 inches of oil in pot to 350°F. Cook chestnuts in hot oil at least 5 minutes. Cool. Remove shells and skins. Chop coarsely. Melt remaining butter in small skillet. Saute nuts gently until browned and cooked through. Place sprouts in prepared shell. Strew nuts over them. Pour on custard. Bake in preheated 375°F. oven 35-45 minutes, or until custard has set completely, is nicely puffed and brown. Allow to stand 3-4 minutes.

Pastry recipes on pages 8-11 Custards on page 13

GLAZED CARROT QUICHE

Quiche pastry
Custard
3-4 whole, peeled carrots
1 tsp. salt
1 tsp. sugar
2 tbs. butter
salt, pepper, nutmeg
2-3 tbs. sugar

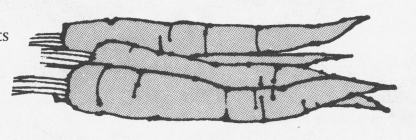

25

Cook the carrots whole in boiling water with salt and sugar until tender. Drain. Slice as thinly as possible. Melt butter in skillet. Add carrots. Season with salt, pepper and nutmeg. Sprinkle remaining sugar over carrots. Toss until well coated. Allow to cook slowly until nicely glazed. Turn occasionally. Place glazed carrots in prepared quiche shell. Pour over custard. Bake in preheated 375°F. oven 35-45 minutes, or until custard is nicely set and tests done in center.

Pastry recipes on pages 8-11   Custards on page 13

SWEET CORN QUICHE

Quiche pastry
Custard
6 ears tender, fresh corn*
1/2 cup milk
3 tbs. sugar
1 tsp. salt
salt and pepper

26

Remove husks and silk from corn. Have ready a large kettleful of boiling water. Add milk, sugar and salt. Add corn, one ear at a time so boiling does not stop. Cook rapidly for 3 minutes. Remove from water. Drain thoroughly. Cut all the kernels from cob. Season with salt and pepper. Put corn in prepared quiche shell. Pour on custard. Bake in preheated 375°F. oven 35-45 minutes, or until custard is completely set and nicely browned. Allow to rest 3-4 minutes before serving. *If fresh corn is not available, 1 16-oz. can well-drained whole kernel corn may be used successfully.

Pastry recipes on pages 8-11 Custards on page 13

SWEET CORN & BACON QUICHE

Follow recipe for Sweet Corn Quiche. Add 1/2 lb. crisply fried, crumbled bacon to corn. Season to taste with salt and pepper. Put into prepared quiche shell. Pour on custard. Bake as directed.

SUCCOTASH QUICHE

Prepare recipe for Sweet Corn Quiche. Cook 2 packages baby lima beans according to package directions. Season with butter. Mix with corn. Put into prepared quiche shell. Pour on custard. Bake as directed.

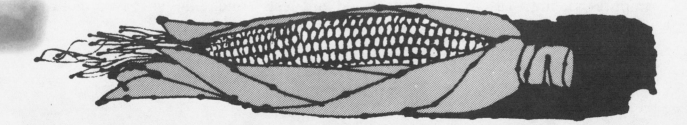

CRAB & AVOCADO QUICHE

Quiche pastry
Custard
1 avocado
lemon juice
salt and pepper
1/2 lb. fresh crab meat
28 1 tsp. Dijon mustard

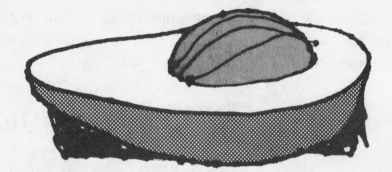

Peel avocado. Cut into 1/2-inch cubes. Sprinkle with lemon juice. Season highly with salt and pepper. Mix quickly with crab. Add mustard. Mix well. Put into prepared quiche shell. Pour on custard. Bake in preheated 375°F. oven 35-45 minutes, or until custard is set, browned and tests done. Allow to rest 5 minutes before serving.

Pastry recipes on pages 8-11   Custards on page 13

JERUSALEM ARTICHOKE QUICHE

Quiche pastry
Custard
6 firm Jerusalem artichokes*
2-3 tbs. butter
salt and pepper

Peel artichokes: Cook in boiling salted water until barely tender when tested with fork. Drain and shake in pot over heat to drive off excess moisture. Slice about 1/4-inch thick. Melt butter in pot. Add slices and toss until well coated with butter. Season with salt and pepper. Place in prepared quiche shell. Pour custard over all. Bake in preheated 375°F. oven 35-45 minutes, or until custard is completely set and thoroughly browned on top. Allow to stand for at least 3 minutes if quiche is to be removed from pan.
*Jerusalem artichokes have, of late, been given the nick-name of "Sunchokes." They are a root, resembling ginger in appearance and Globe artichokes in flavor.

Pastry recipes on pages 8-11   Custards on page 13

MUSHROOM QUICHE

Quiche pastry   1/2 lb. mushrooms   salt, pepper, rosemary
Custard   clarified butter*

    Wash mushrooms. Remove stems. Cut caps in quarters. *Melt 3 tablespoons butter over gentle heat. Strain off clear butter, discarding white solids left in pan. Cook mushrooms over very high heat in smoking clarified butter. They must be thoroughly fried with no moisture remaining. Season to taste with salt, pepper and a little rosemary. Put into quiche shell. Pour on custard. Bake in preheated 375°F. oven 40-45 minutes, or until custard has set completely.

31

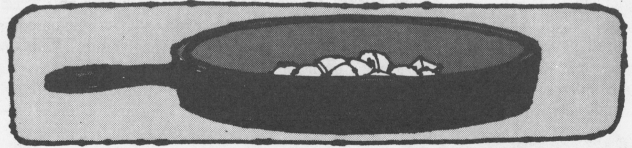

Pastry recipes on pages 8-11 Custards on page 13

MUSHROOM & GREEN PEPPER QUICHE

Quiche pastry
Custard
1/2 lb. mushrooms
clarified butter*
2 green peppers
salt, freshly ground pepper

32

   Wash and thoroughly dry mushrooms. Remove stems and slice. *Melt 3 tablespoons butter over gentle heat. Strain off clear butter, discarding white solids left in pan. Saute mushrooms briskly in smoking-hot, clarified butter until crisp and brown. Slice peppers into small pieces. Add to mushrooms. Continue cooking until peppers are soft. Season to taste. Put mixture into quiche shell. Pour on custard. Bake in preheated 375°F. oven 35-40 minutes, or until custard has set completely and is nicely browned. Allow to stand 3-4 minutes before serving, especially if it is to be unmolded.

Pastry recipes on pages 8-11   Custards on page 13

MUSHROOM & STRING BEAN QUICHE

Quiche pastry
Custard
1/2 lb. mushrooms
clarified butter*
1/2 lb. French cut string beans
1 tbs. butter
salt, pepper, basil

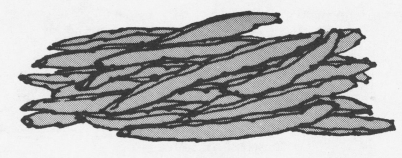

Wash and dry mushrooms. Remove stems and slice. *Melt 3 tablespoons butter over gentle heat. Strain off clear butter, discarding white solids left in pan. Saute mushrooms briskly in smoking-hot, clarified butter until crisp and brown. Prepare string beans as described in the Paul Mayer Method for cooking green vegetables on page 19. Butter beans. Combine with mushrooms. Season to taste with salt, pepper and basil. Turn mixture into quiche shell. Pour on custard. Bake in preheated 375°F. oven 40-45 minutes, or until custard is set and deeply browned. Allow to rest 4-5 minutes before serving.

Pastry recipes on pages 8-11   Custards on page 13

MUSHROOM & SOUR CREAM QUICHE

Quiche pastry
1 cup sour cream
4 egg yolks
salt, cayenne
1/2 lb. mushrooms
clarified butter*
1-1/2 tsp. Worcestershire sauce

34

Beat sour cream, egg yolks, salt and cayenne together in bowl. Wash trim and slice mushrooms. *Melt 3 tablespoons butter over gentle heat. Strain off clear butter, discarding white solids left in pan. Saute mushrooms briskly in smoking-hot, clarified butter until crisp and brown. Add Worcestershire sauce. Continue cooking until sauce has all evaporated. Fill prepared quiche shell. Pour on sour cream custard. Bake 40-45 minutes in preheated 375°F. oven, or until custard is thoroughly set and nicely browned on top. Allow to rest 3-4 minutes before serving.

Pastry recipes on pages 8-11 Custards on page 13

ONION QUICHE

Quiche pastry
Custard
4 or 5 medium onions

1/4 cup butter
salt, freshly ground pepper
2 tsp. paprika

Peel and slice onions. Melt butter in heavy skillet. Saute onions slowly until they are soft and brown, and all moisture has cooked away. Season highly with salt, pepper and paprika. Place onions in quiche shell. Pour on custard. Bake in preheated 375°F. oven 35-45 minutes, or until custard has set completely and is deeply browned. Allow to rest 4-5 minutes before removing to serving dish.

35

Pastry recipes on pages 8-11   Custards on page 13

POTATO QUICHE

| Quiche pastry | 2 lbs. boiling potatoes | 1 medium onion |
| Custard | salt, pepper | 6 tbs. butter |

Peel and thinly slice potatoes and onion. Season with salt and pepper. Melt butter in skillet. Add potato and onion slices. Cook over moderate heat until onions are soft and potatoes are crisp and browned. Fill quiche shell with mixture. Pour on custard. Bake in preheated 375°F. oven 40-45 minutes, or until custard tests done.

36

POTATO & HARD-COOKED EGG QUICHE

Follow directions for making Potato Quiche. Add 1 coarsely chopped hard-cooked egg. Fill quiche shell with mixture. Pour on custard. Bake in preheated 375°F. oven 40-45 minutes, or until custard tests done and surface is deeply browned.

Pastry recipes on pages 8-11   Custards on page 13

POTATO-EGG & BACON QUICHE

Follow directions for making Potato Quiche. Add 1 coarsely chopped hard-cooked egg and 6 slices crisp bacon which have been crumbled, to the potato-onion mixture. Turn into shell. Pour on custard. Bake in preheated 375° F. oven as directed.

SAUERKRAUT QUICHE

Quiche pastry
Custard
1 can (16-oz.) sauerkraut

2 tbs. butter or lard
1 tbs. caraway
salt, freshly ground pepper

Thoroughly drain sauerkraut. Squeeze well to remove all liquid. Heat fat in deep saucepan. When hot add kraut and remaining ingredients. Cook until all moisture cooks away and sauerkraut is greasy in appearance. Put into prepared quiche shell. Pour on custard. Bake in preheated 375°F. oven 40-50 minutes, or until custard is set and pastry well browned. Allow to set 3-4 minutes before serving.

SAUERKRAUT & SAUSAGE QUICHE

Prepare recipe for Sauerkraut Quiche. Place half of kraut mixture in shell. Cover with layer of sliced garlic sausage. Top with remaining kraut. Pour on custard. Bake as directed.

Pastry recipes on pages 8-11 Custards on page 13

FRESH SPINACH QUICHE

Quiche pastry   2 lbs. fresh spinach   salt & pepper
Custard   1/4 cup melted butter

Wash spinach several times. Cook in large pot over high heat, using only water which clings to leaves after final washing. As soon as spinach is completely wilted, remove from heat. Drain thoroughly. Squeeze small handsful as hard as possible to eliminate all moisture. Add melted butter. Season well. Fill prepared quiche shell with spinach. Pour on custard. Bake in preheated 375°F. oven 40-45 minutes, or until custard is set and pastry well browned. Allow to set 3-4 minutes before serving.

40

Pastry recipes on pages 8-11   Custards on page 13

FRESH SPINACH & CHEESE QUICHE

Quiche pastry
Custard
2 lbs. fresh spinach
1/4 cup melted butter
salt & pepper
1 cup grated Gruyere cheese

Wash spinach several times. Cook in large pot over high heat, using only water which clings to leaves after final washing. As soon as spinach is completely wilted, remove from heat. Drain thoroughly. Squeeze small handsful as hard as possible to eliminate all moisture. Add melted butter. Season. Stir in cheese. Fill prepared quiche shell. Pour over custard. Bake in preheated 375°F. oven 40-45 minutes, or until custard is set and pastry browned. Allow to rest 3-4 minutes before serving.

Pastry recipes on pages 8-11   Custards on page 13

FRESH SPINACH & SOUR CREAM QUICHE

1 cup sour cream
4 egg yolks
salt, cayenne, nutmeg
2 lbs. fresh spinach
1/4 cup melted butter
salt, pepper

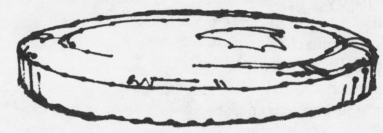

42

Beat sour cream, egg yolks, salt, cayenne and nutmeg together in bowl. Wash spinach very well. Cook in large pot over high heat using only water which clings to leaves from final washing. When spinach is completely wilted, remove from heat. Drain. Squeeze small handsful as hard as possible to eliminate all moisture. Toss with butter and seasonings. Place in prepared quiche shell. Pour on custard. Bake in preheated 375°F. oven 40-45 minutes, or until custard tests done and pastry is nicely browned. Allow to stand 3-4 minutes before serving.

Pastry recipes on pages 8-11   Custards on page 13

TOMATO & EGGPLANT QUICHE

Quiche pastry
Custard
1 small eggplant
salt, flour
1 egg, beaten

dried bread crumbs
oil for frying
2 small tomatoes
salt, pepper, basil

Slice unpeeled eggplant. Score the surface of slices with fork. Sprinkle with salt. Allow to stand 15 minutes or until moisture rises to surface and can be wiped away. Flour slices. Mix a little water with egg. Dip floured slices in egg then coat thoroughly with crumbs. Heat oil to 380°F. Fry eggplant until crisp and deeply browned. Remove to paper towel to drain. Peel and slice tomatoes. Hold slices under running water to rinse away all seeds and jelly. Pat dry. Place a layer of eggplant slices in prepared quiche shell. Season with salt, pepper and a little basil. Cover with a layer of tomato slices. Season. Continue until the shell is filled. Pour on custard. Bake in preheated 375°F. oven 40-45 minutes, or until custard tests done. Allow to stand about 5 minutes before serving.

43

Pastry recipes on pages 8-11   Custards on page 13

QUICHES WITH EGGS

Perhaps quiches made with eggs as the filling are a redundancy, yet this happy combination of eggs and custard proves to be delicious and a fine beginning for several other combination fillings as well. Probably more at home on the luncheon or brunch table, these next several quiches will do beautifully baked in an 8 or 9-inch square pan and cut into small tidbits for cocktail-time tarrying.

SLICED EGG & ONION QUICHE

Quiche pastry
Custard
2 large sweet onions
3 tbs. butter
salt, freshly ground pepper
1 tsp. paprika
4 hard cooked eggs*

46

Peel and slice onions. Melt butter in skillet. Add onions, salt and pepper. Cook over moderate heat until onions are very soft. Add paprika. Slice eggs. Place a layer of eggs in bottom of prepared quiche shell. Spread a spoonful of onion over eggs. Continue layering until eggs and onions are used. End with layer of eggs on top. Pour on custard. Bake in preheated 375°F. oven 40-45 minutes, or until custard tests done and pastry is nicely browned. Allow to set 3-4 minutes before serving. *See page 47.

Pastry recipes on pages 8-11   Custards on page 13

SLICED EGG & SMOKED SALMON QUICHE

Quiche pastry
Custard
4 hard-cooked eggs*
1/4 lb. thinly sliced smoked salmon
freshly ground pepper

Slice eggs. Place a layer in bottom of prepared quiche shell. Cover with layer of salmon. Season well with pepper. Continue layering until shell is filled. End with eggs on top. Pour on custard. Bake in preheated 375°F. oven 35-40 minutes, or until custard tests done and pastry is nicely browned. Let rest 3-4 minutes before serving. *To hard cook a proper egg—Place in cold water. Bring slowly to boil. Simmer, *do not boil,* 25 minutes. Crack shells immediately when cooking time is up. Run cold water over them several minutes. Shell under running water. Dry with paper towel. When eggs are cooked this way, the yolks stay bright yellow and they look pretty when sliced.

Pastry recipes on pages 8-11   Custards on page 13

SLICED EGG & BACON QUICHE

Quiche pastry
Custard
1/2 lb. bacon
4 hard-cooked eggs*

48 Cook bacon until very crisp. Drain thoroughly. Slice eggs. Place a slice of bacon in prepared quiche shell. Lean 3-4 egg slices against bacon. Place another slice of bacon alongside egg slices. Then another row of eggs and another piece of bacon. Continue in this fashion until shell is filled. Pour on custard. Bake in preheated 375°F. oven 40-45 minutes, or until custard tests done and pastry is nicely browned. Allow to stand 3-4 minutes before serving. *See page 47.

Pastry recipes on pages 8-11   Custards on page 13

SLICED EGG & HAM QUICHE

Quiche pastry   mustard
Custard   4 hard-cooked eggs*
1/2 lb. boiled ham slices

    Spread ham slices with mustard. Cut into small pieces. Slice eggs. Place a layer of egg slices in bottom of prepared quiche shell. Sprinkle with a spoonful of ham pieces. Cover ham with more egg slices. Continue layering until shell is filled. Pour on custard. Bake in preheated 375°F. oven 40-45 minutes, or until custard tests done and pastry is nicely browned. Allow to stand 3-4 minutes before serving. *See page 47.

49

SLICED EGG & SALAMI QUICHE

    Follow recipe for Sliced Egg & Ham Quiche, substituting thin slices of salami for boiled ham.

Pastry recipes on pages 8-11   Custards on page 13

EGG & TONGUE QUICHE

Follow recipe for Sliced Egg & Ham Quiche, substituting tongue slices for ham. Bake as directed.

EGG & ROAST BEEF QUICHE

50 Follow recipe for Sliced Egg & Ham Quiche, but substitute thin slices of rare roast beef for the ham.

EGG & SMOKED TURKEY QUICHE

Follow recipe for Sliced Egg & Ham Quiche, substituting thin slices of smoked turkey for the ham.

SLICED EGG & CHICKEN LIVER QUICHE

Quiche pastry
Custard
clarified butter*
1/2 lb. chicken livers

2 tbs. butter
1 large finely chopped onion
fresh pepper, pinch coriander
4 hard-cooked eggs**

*Melt 3 tablespoons butter over gentle heat. Strain off clear butter, discarding white solids left in pan. Cook chicken livers in clarified butter over very high heat until nicely browned. Avoid overcooking as this toughens the livers. Remove from pan. Add 2 tablespoons butter to pan. When melted, saute onion until nicely browned. Slice livers and return to pan. Season. Slice eggs. Place layer of egg slices in bottom of prepared quiche shell. Spread some of liver mixture over eggs. Continue layering until shell is filled. End with eggs on top. Pour on custard. Bake in preheated 375°F. oven 40-45 minutes, or until custard tests done and pastry is nicely browned. Allow to set 3-4 minutes before serving. **See page 47.

51

Pastry recipes on pages 8-11   Custards on page 13

DEVILED EGG & BACON QUICHE

Quiche pastry
Custard
4 hard cooked eggs*
6 slices crisply fried bacon
salt, pepper
Dijon mustard
grated onion
mayonnaise

53

Cut eggs in half lengthwise. Remove yolks. Force through strainer. Mix with crumbled bacon. Season with salt, pepper, mustard, onion and only enough mayonnaise to make a very firm mixture. Pack into whites, filling them flush. Place eggs, stuffed-side up, in prepared quiche shell. Pour on custard. Bake in preheated 375°F. oven 40-45 minutes, or until custard tests done and crust is nicely browned. Allow to stand 4-5 minutes before serving. *See page 47.

Pastry recipes on pages 8-11   Custards on page 13

DEVILED EGG & PIMIENTO QUICHE

Follow recipe for Deviled Egg & Bacon Quiche. Substitute 2 cans of whole pimientos finely chopped, for the bacon.

DEVILED EGG & CAPER QUICHE

54   Follow recipe for Deviled Egg & Bacon Quiche. Substitute 1 small jar of finely chopped capers for the bacon.

DEVILED EGG & BLACK OLIVE QUICHE

Follow recipe for Deviled Egg & Bacon Quiche. Substitute 3 tablespoons finely chopped black olives for the bacon.

QUICHES WITH FISH

Menus have long been studded with all sorts of things done up in patty shells, but only recently have people started considering the possibilities that could be combined in a tart or quiche shell. So far, we have looked at the way vegetables and eggs lend themselves to presentation in this fashion, but what of meats, fish, and poultry? Long standing as an almost over-trite luncheon offering is the ubiquitous "Creamed Chicken & Green Peas in a Patty Shell"—the almost unfailing sign of "no imagination" menu planning.

But why not the quiche? It is easy to prepare ahead of time and actually requires less "final moment" doing than even filling those verdammte patty shells. If you use pretty porcelain quiche dishes, the finished product can be carted directly from the oven to the table. With the addition of hot rolls and a crisp intriguing salad, you can make a truly conversation stopping luncheon. Coming up then, are only a few of the hundreds of ways of using fish—(and later on meats and poultry) in quiches. Having these as a guide, you will be able to dream up many fine seafood quiche fillings.

FINNAN HADDIE QUICHE

Quiche pastry   1 lb. finnan haddie   salt, Tabasco
Custard   1/4 cup melted butter

Soak finnan haddie in cold water for several hours. Change the water twice during soaking period. Place fish in deep saucepan. Cover with water. Bring slowly to boil. Pour off water and start again. When water boils a second time, reduce heat. Simmer fish 10 to 15 minutes, or until cooked and tender. Drain thoroughly. Mix with butter, salt and a little Tabasco. Place buttered fish in prepared quiche shell. Pour on custard. Bake in preheated 375° F. oven 35-40 minutes, or until custard tests done and pastry is nicely browned. Allow to stand 3-4 minutes before serving.

56

Pastry recipes on pages 8-11 Custards on page 13

SMOKED SALMON QUICHE

Quiche pastry
Custard
1/4 lb. thinly sliced smoked salmon

Pour custard into prepared shell first! *This is a departure from the usual way of making quiche.* Then carefully float enough salmon slices to cover the surface. With a teaspoon lift some of the custard over top of salmon. Work carefully so slices do not sink all the way to the bottom of the shell. Bake in preheated 375°F. oven 40-45 minutes, or until custard is set and pastry nicely browned. Allow to stand 3-4 minutes before serving.

57

Pastry recipes on pages 8-11   Custards on page 13

CRAB QUICHE

Quiche pastry   1/2 lb. crab meat
Custard   2 tbs. Sherry, warmed
2 tbs. butter

58   Melt butter. Add crab meat. Toss until well coated with butter. Pour on sherry. Set ablaze. When flame dies out, continue cooking gently until liquid has completely evaporated. Put crab meat into prepared quiche shell. Pour on custard. Bake in preheated 375°F. oven 35-40 minutes, or until custard tests done and pastry is nicely browned. Allow to stand 3-4 minutes before serving.

CRAB & PIMIENTO QUICHE

Follow recipe for Crab Quiche. Add 1 small can chopped pimiento to crab meat before cooking in butter.

Pastry recipes on pages 8-11   Custards on page 13

SHRIMP QUICHE

Quiche pastry
Custard
1/2 lb. cooked, shelled shrimp

If shrimp are not cooked, place unshelled in a pan of cold water. Add 3-4 whole peppercorns, a bay leaf and 1/4 cup dry white wine. Place over moderate heat. Bring slowly to boil. As soon as water boils discard it. Immediately rinse shrimp in cold water to stop further cooking. Shell and devein. If shrimp are large, cut into small pieces. Fill prepared quiche shell with shrimp. Pour on custard. Bake in preheated 375°F. oven 40-45 minutes, or until custard is set and pastry is nicely browned. Allow to rest 3-4 minutes before serving.

Pastry recipes on pages 8-11   Custards on page 13

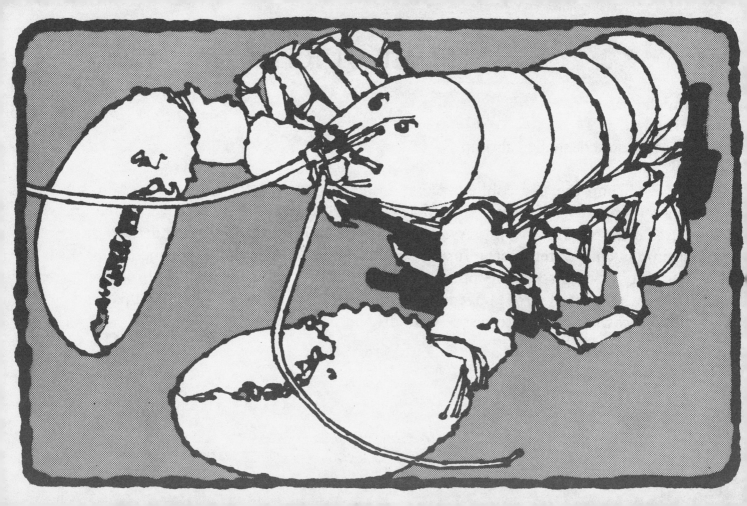

SHRIMP NEWBURG QUICHE

There is a story that tells how the original Sauce Newburg was invented by a chef in honor of a renowned gourmet named Wenburg, but after the two had quarreled seriously, the chef reneged on his promise to name the new creation after his patron, and so reversed the first three letters of the name!

To make Shrimp Newburg Quiche, follow the recipe for Shrimp Quiche. Add 1 extra egg yolk and 1/4 cup sherry to custard ingredients.

LOBSTER QUICHE

Follow recipe for Shrimp Quiche, using lobster meat instead of shrimp. If you live in the East, by all means use fresh eastern lobster. Cook as described for shrimp in the Shrimp Quiche recipe, except allow lobster to simmer gently 5 minutes after it reaches boiling. Remove meat and chop into small pieces.

LOBSTER THERMIDOR QUICHE

Quiche pastry
Custard
1/2 lb. lobster meat
3 tbs. butter
1 finely chopped onion
1/2 cup dry white wine
3 tbs. grated Parmesan cheese

Chop lobster meat coarsely. Melt butter in skillet. Saute onion in butter until soft, but do not allow to color at all. Add wine. Simmer until liquid has all cooked away. Add lobster meat and Parmesan. Toss all together. Put into prepared quiche shell. Pour on custard. Bake in preheated 375°F. oven 40-45 minutes, or until custard tests done and pastry is nicely browned. Allow to set 3-4 minutes before serving.

Pastry recipes on pages 8-11   Custards on page 13

QUICHE A LA SOLE MARGUERY

Quiche pastry
Custard
6 fillets of sole
3/4 cup dry white wine
1/2 cup water
salt
3-4 whole peppercorns

1 bay leaf
1/4 lb. mushrooms, sliced
3 tbs. butter
1/4 lb. tiny shrimp
1 jar well-drained mussels
1 tbs. finely chopped parsley

Fold sole in half lengthwise. Place in lightly buttered baking dish. Combine wine, water, a little salt, peppercorns and bay leaf. Pour over fish. Cover closely with waxed paper. Bake in 350°F. oven 12 minutes. Drain fish. Dry thoroughly with paper towel. Arrange cooked fish, spoke-fashion, in prepared quiche shell. Saute mushrooms in butter over high heat until crisp and browned. Add shrimp and mussels. Season with salt and pepper. Add parsley. Spread over fish. Pour on custard. Bake in preheated 375°F. oven 40-45 minutes, or until custard tests done and pastry is nicely browned. Allow to rest 3-4 minutes before serving.

Pastry recipes on pages 8-11   Custards on page 13

QUICHE A LA SOLE DUGLERE

Quiche pastry
Custard
6 fillets of sole
3/4 cup dry white wine
1/2 cup water

3-4 peppercorns
1 bay leaf
1 large tomato
2 tbs. parsley
1 tbs. grated Parmesan cheese

64

Fold sole in half lengthwise. Place in lightly buttered baking dish. Combine wine, water, a little salt, peppercorns and bay leaf. Pour over fish. Cover closely with waxed paper. Bake in 350°F. oven 12 minutes. Drain fish. Dry thoroughly with paper towel. Arrange cooked fish, spoke-fashion, in prepared quiche shell. Peel tomato by dipping in boiling water 10 seconds. Plunge into cold water. Slip off skin. Cut in quarters. Remove center section. Cut remaining tomato shell into thin lengthwise strips. Scatter over fish. Sprinkle with parsley and cheese. Pour over custard. Bake in preheated 375°F. oven 40-45 minutes, or until custard tests done and quiche shell is well browned. Allow to stand 3-4 minutes before serving.

Pastry recipes on pages 8-11   Custards on page 13

QUICHE A LA SOLE BANGKOK

Quiche pastry
Custard with 1/2 tsp. curry powder added
6 small fillets of sole
3/4 cup dry white wine
1/2 cup water
3-4 peppercorns

1 bay leaf
1/4 lb. mushrooms
3 tbs. butter
3-4 pieces preserved ginger
1/4 cup walnuts
1/4 lb. tiny shrimp

Fold sole in half lengthwise. Place in lightly buttered baking dish. Combine wine, water, a little salt, peppercorns and bay leaf. Pour over fish. Cover closely with waxed paper. Bake in 350°F. oven 12 minutes. Drain fish. Dry thoroughly with paper towel. Arrange cooked fish, spoke-fashion, in prepared quiche shell. Slice mushrooms. Fry briskly in butter until crisp and brown. Cut ginger into thick slices. Finely chop walnuts. Mix with shrimp. Spread over sole. Pour on Curry-Custard. Bake in preheated 375°F. oven 40-45 minutes, or until custard tests done and pastry is nicely browned. Allow to stand 3-4 minutes before serving.

65

Pastry recipes on pages 8-11   Custards on page 13

QUICHE A LA SOLE NEW ORLEANS

Quiche pastry
Custard—substitute 1 cup
    sour cream in custard B
6 small fillets of sole

3/4 cup dry white wine
1/2 cup water
3-4 peppercorns

1 bay leaf
1 bunch fresh spinach
1 large, ripe tomato

Fold sole in half lengthwise. Place in lightly buttered baking dish. Combine wine, water, a little salt, peppercorns and bay leaf. Pour over fish. Cover closely with waxed paper. Bake in 350°F oven 12 minutes. Drain fish. Dry thoroughly with paper towel. Arrange cooked fish, spoke-fashion, in prepared quiche shell. Thoroughly wash spinach. Cook over high heat using only water clinging to leaves. When wilted completely, drain well. Squeeze small handsful until absolutely water-free. Mix with melted butter. Season with salt and pepper. Spread over fish. Dip tomato in boiling water for 10 seconds. Plunge into cold water. Slip off skin. Slice peeled tomato. Hold slices under running water to flush away seeds and jelly. Dry slices. Place on top of spinach. Pour on custard. Bake in preheated 375°F. oven 40-45 minutes, or until custard tests done and pastry is nicely browned. Allow to set 3-4 minutes before serving.

Pastry recipes on pages 8-11 Custards on page 13

SOLE & SMOKED SALMON QUICHE

Quiche pastry
Custard
6 small fillets of sole
3/4 cup white wine
1/2 cup water
3-4 whole peppercorns
1 bay leaf
1/4 lb. smoked salmon

68

Fold sole in half lengthwise. Place in lightly buttered baking dish. Pour wine, and water over fish. Sprinkle with a little salt. Add peppercorns and bay leaf. Cover fish closely with waxed paper. Bake 12 minutes in 350°F. oven. Drain fish. Dry thoroughly on paper towel. Arrange cooked sole spoke-fashion in prepared quiche shell. Chop salmon coarsely. Sprinkle between fillets. Pour over custard. Bake in preheated 375°F. oven 40-45 minutes, or until custard is set and pastry well-browned. Allow to rest 3-4 minutes before serving.

Pastry recipes on pages 8-11   Custards on page 13

QUICHES WITH MEAT & POULTRY

Whereas quiches are primarily used for luncheons or as accompaniments to meats, several types can be made featuring meat or poultry and once again, the range seems to be limited largely to one's imagination. As a guide, here are only a few from which, perhaps, your own fancies will take flight and lead you to many others even more interesting. And don't forget quiches when entertaining! They take the Busy-Hostess-Award for being impressive and delicious with a minimum of effort. They are exciting to look at, so good to eat and require almost no last minute attention. Everything can be prepared ahead of time and quickly assembled just before being put into the oven. Either as the main attraction with salad and a good bottle of wine, or as a hot hors d'oeuvre your guests will love quiches and you, too, for serving them. And, merely as an aside to some of the many airlines—I should think that the quiche would lend itself admirably to in-flight preparation. Since the various components could be prepared beforehand on the ground and placed aboard the aircraft, the Coffeeteaormilks would only have to pour the custard over, and put them to bake, which shouldn't put too much of a burden on their culinary capacities.

CHICKEN A LA KING QUICHE

Quiche pastry
Custard
1 onion
1 green pepper
2 tbs. butter
1 small can chopped pimiento
2 cups cooked chicken
1/4 cup Sherry, warmed

Chop onion. Cut pepper in small chunks. Melt butter in skillet. Add onion, pepper and pimiento. Cook until soft. Cut chicken same as green pepper. Mix with vegetables. Pour on warmed Sherry. Ignite. When flame dies out, continue cooking over brisk heat until wine has completely evaporated. Put into prepared pastry shell. Pour on custard. Bake in preheated 375°F. oven 35-40 minutes, or until custard tests done and pastry is nicely browned. Allow to set 3-4 minutes before serving.

Pastry recipes on pages 8-11 Custards on page 13

QUICHE A LA CHICKEN KIEV

Quiche pastry
Custard
2 cups cooked chicken pieces

3 tbs. melted butter
1 tbs. finely chopped parsley
1 clove garlic, pressed

Saute chicken in butter until brown. Sprinkle parsley and garlic over chicken. Pour on custard. Bake in preheated 375° F. oven 35-40 minutes, or until custard tests done and pastry is nicely browned. Allow to stand 3-4 minutes before serving.

CHICKEN & MUSHROOM QUICHE

Follow recipe for Quiche a la Chicken Kiev. Use only 1 cup chicken. Omit parsley and garlic. Saute 1/2 pound finely sliced mushrooms in butter over high heat until brown. Stir in chicken. Put into shell. Pour on custard. Bake as directed.

Pastry recipes on pages 8-11   Custards on page 13

CHICKEN HASH QUICHE

Quiche pastry
Custard
1 cup cooked chicken
3 new, red potatoes
1 onion

3 tbs. butter
salt, pepper
1/2 tsp. Worcestershire sauce
1 tsp. Dijon mustard

Cut chicken into small cubes. Boil potatoes in salted water until tender. Peel. Cut in cubes same size as chicken. Finely chop onion. Melt butter in skillet. Add chicken, potatoes and onion. Saute over medium heat until onion is soft and mixture nicely browned. Season with salt, pepper, Worcestershire sauce and mustard. Put into prepared quiche shell. Pour on custard. Bake in preheated 375°F. oven 40-45 minutes, or until custard tests done and pastry is nicely browned. Allow to rest 3-4 minutes before serving.

73

Pastry recipes on pages 8-11   Custards on page 13

CHICKEN & OLIVE QUICHE

Quiche pastry
Custard
2 cups cooked chicken

salt, black pepper
1/2 cup chopped black olives

Cut chicken into cubes. Season with salt and pepper. Put into prepared quiche shell. Scatter olives over chicken. Pour on custard. Bake in preheated 375°F. oven 40-45 minutes, or until custard is set and tests done and pastry is nicely browned. Allow to rest 3-4 minutes before serving.

74

SMOKED TURKEY QUICHE

Pour custard into prepared quiche shell first. Carefully float enough turkey slices to cover surface of custard. Gently spoon a little custard over turkey. Bake in preheated 375°F. oven 35-40 minutes, or until custard tests done. Allow to stand 3-4 minutes before serving.

Pastry recipes on pages 8-11   Custards on page 13

KIDNEY & MUSHROOM QUICHE

Quiche pastry
Custard
7 or 8 small veal kidneys
4 tbs. clarified butter*
2-3 tbs. brandy, warmed

1/4 lb. mushrooms, finely sliced
salt, pepper
1/2 tsp. dry mustard
1 tsp. water

Remove core from kidneys. Cut into small pieces. *Melt butter over gentle heat. Strain off clear butter, discarding white solids left in pan. Heat 2 tablespoons clarified butter in skillet until it smokes. Keep heat at its highest. Add kidneys. Brown quickly on all sides. Pour on warmed brandy. Ignite. When flame goes out, remove kidneys from pan. Add remaining butter to pan. Over high heat, saute mushrooms until nicely browned. Add kidneys, salt, pepper and mustard which has been dissolved in water. Put into prepared quiche shell. Pour on custard. Bake in preheated 375°F. oven 35-40 minutes, or until custard tests done and pastry is nicely browned. Allow to rest 3-4 minutes before serving.

Pastry recipes on pages 8-11   Custards on page 13

STEAK & KIDNEY QUICHE

Quiche pastry
Custard
1 lb. tenderloin tips
4 tbs. clarified butter*
5-6 small veal kidneys
1 small onion, grated
salt, pepper

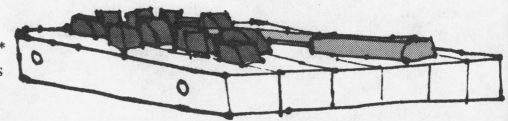

76

Cut tenderloin tips into small chunks. *Melt butter over gentle heat. Strain off clear butter, discarding white solids left in pan. Heat 2 tablespoons clarified butter in skillet until it smokes. Keep heat at its highest. Brown tips. Remove from pan. Add remaining clarified butter to skillet. Heat to smoking. Add kidneys. Brown quickly. Combine tips, kidneys and onion. Season. Fill prepared quiche shell. Pour on custard. Bake in preheated 375°F. oven 40-45 minutes, or until custard tests done and pastry is nicely browned. Allow to rest 3-4 minutes before serving.

Pastry recipes on pages 8-11   Custards on page 13

STEAK & ONION QUICHE

Quiche pastry
Custard
1 lb. tenderloin tips
4 tbs. clarified butter*
4 medium onions
salt, pepper

Cut tenderloin tips into small chunks. *Melt butter over gentle heat. Strain off clear butter, discarding white solids left in pan. Heat 2 tablespoons clarified butter in skillet until it smokes. Keep heat at its highest. Brown tips. Remove from pan. Lower heat. Add remaining butter to pan. Slice onions thin. Add to heated butter. Cook until soft and starting to brown. Add beef. Season well with salt and freshly ground pepper. Put into prepared quiche shell. Pour on custard. Bake in preheated 375°F. oven 40-45 minutes or until custard is set and pastry nicely browned. Allow to rest 3-4 minutes before serving.

Pastry recipes on pages 8-11   Custards on page 13

BEEF STROGANOFF QUICHE

Quiche pastry
1 cup sour cream
2 whole eggs
1 egg yolk

salt, pepper
1 lb. tenderloin tips
4 tbs. clarified butter*
2 tbs. brandy, warmed

1 clove garlic
1/4 lb. mushrooms, sliced

Measure sour cream into mixing bowl. Add eggs, egg yolk, salt and pepper. Stir until well blended and mixture is smooth. Set aside. Cut tenderloin tips into finger lengths. *Melt butter over gentle heat. Strain off clear butter, discarding the white solids left in pan. Heat 2 tablespoons clarified butter in large skillet until very hot. Quickly brown tips. Pour on warmed brandy. Ignite. When flame goes out, remove meat from skillet. Lower heat. Add remaining 2 tablespoons clarified butter. Press garlic. Add to butter. Cook slowly for 1 minute. Increase heat to high. Add mushrooms. Brown quickly. Add tips. Mix well with mushrooms. Spoon into bottom of prepared shell. Pour custard mixture over top. Bake in preheated 375° F. oven 40-45 minutes, or until custard is set and pastry nicely browned. Allow to rest for 3-4 minutes before serving.

79

Pastry recipes on pages 8-11   Custards on page 13

QUICHE A LA BLANQUETTE DE VEAU

Quiche pastry
Custard
1/4 lb. boneless veal shoulder
1 small onion, sliced
1/2 carrot, sliced

1/2 stalk celery, sliced
1/2 tsp. salt
24 tiniest onions
1/4 lb. mushrooms
2 tbs. butter

80

Cut veal into small cubes. Place in saucepan. Cover with cold water. Bring slowly to boil. Drain. Rinse in cold water. Wash saucepan. Return veal to saucepan with onion, carrot, celery and salt. Barely cover with cold water. Bring to boil. Lower heat. Simmer gently until meat is tender, 30-45 minutes. Boil tiny onions in salted water until tender. Cut mushrooms into quarters. Saute in butter until browned and free from moisture. Drain and dry onions. Combine with mushrooms. When meat is tender, drain and dry on paper towels. Toss meat with mushrooms and onions. Fill prepared quiche shell. Pour on custard. Bake in preheated 375°F. oven 40-45 minutes, or until well browned and tests done. Allow to rest 3-4 minutes before serving.

Pastry recipes on pages 8-11   Custards on page 13

VEAL & GREEN PEPPER QUICHE

Quiche pastry
Custard
1/4 lb. boneless veal shoulder
1 small onion, sliced
1/2 carrot, sliced

1/2 stalk celery, sliced
1/2 tsp. salt
3 green peppers
3 tbs. butter
salt, pepper

Cut veal into small cubes. Place in saucepan. Cover with cold water. Bring slowly to boil. Drain. Rinse in cold water. Wash saucepan. Return veal to saucepan with onion, carrot, celery and salt. Barely cover with cold water. Bring to boil. Lower heat. Simmer gently until meat is tender, 30-45 minutes. Cut peppers into strips. Melt butter in skillet. Saute pepper strips over moderate heat until tender. Drain and dry on paper towels. Drain and dry veal. Combine with peppers. Season to taste. Put into prepared quiche shell. Pour on custard. Bake in preheated 375°F. oven 40-45 minutes, or until custard tests done and pastry is nicely browned. Allow to rest 3-4 minutes before serving.

81

Pastry recipes on pages 8-11   Custards on page 13

CHEESEBURGER QUICHE

Quiche pastry   1/2 lb. fat-free ground round
Custard   salt, pepper
2 tbs. butter   1/2 cup grated sharp Cheddar cheese

Melt butter in skillet over high heat. When very hot, fry meat until browned and completely free of moisture. Season with salt and pepper. Place in prepared quiche shell. Spread cheese over meat. Pour on custard. Bake in preheated 375°F. oven 40-45 minutes, or until custard is completely set and pastry is well browned. Allow to rest 3-4 minutes before serving.

82

CHILIBURGER QUICHE

Follow recipe for Cheeseburger Quiche. Sprinkle 1 teaspoon chili powder over grated cheese before pouring on custard. Bake as directed.

Pastry recipes on pages 8-11   Custards on page 13

REUBEN QUICHE

Quiche pastry
Custard
1 can (16-oz.) sauerkraut, drained
2 tbs. butter
1 tsp. caraway seeds
1/4 lb. thinly sliced corned beef
1/4 lb. thinly sliced Gruyere cheese

84

Squeeze small handsful of sauerkraut to extract all moisture. Melt butter in skillet. Saute kraut until it begins to brown and is covered with butter. Add caraway seeds. Put into prepared quiche shell. Place corned beef slices over kraut. Top with cheese slices. Pour on custard. Bake in preheated 375°F. oven 40-45 minutes, or until custard is set and pastry nicely browned. Allow to stand 3-4 minutes before serving.

Pastry recipes on pages 8-11   Custards on page 13

FRANKFURTER QUICHE

Quiche pastry   1/2 lb. frankfurters
Custard

   Slice franks thin. Layer in prepared shell. Pour on custard. Bake in preheated 375°F. oven 40-45 minutes, or until custard tests done and pastry is nicely browned. Allow to rest 3-4 minutes before serving.

FRANKFURTER & BEAN QUICHE

Quiche pastry   1 can (8oz.) baked beans
Custard   1/2 lb. frankfurters, thinly sliced

   Place beans in strainer. Rinse away all sauce. Dry on paper towels. Spread a layer of frankfurters in prepared shell. Top with beans. Cover with rest of franks. Pour on custard. Bake in preheated 375°F. oven 40-45 minutes.

Pastry recipes on pages 8-11   Custards on page 13

INDEX

Souffle

by Paul Mayer

Illustrated by CRAIG TORLUCCI

TABLE OF CONTENTS

UP! UP! AND AWAY!!!

Since man first came down from the trees, it seems he has been trying, in one way or another, to get back up into the air once again. History is studded with examples of man's colossal attempts to reach the sky, once he had reached the ground. The colossus of Rhodes, the Pyramids, Greek and Roman temples, the Hanging Gardens, all pointed the way until man sought a means of leaving the earth without first building a platform to get there.

Even Leonardo da Vinci worked on the problem and left behind a design for a flying machine, but it wasn't until 1783 that the two French brothers—Joseph Michael and Jacques Etienne Montgolfier—rose swiftly and silently from the earth in what was the first practical ascent by balloon and ushered in the Air Age.

However, the Air Age had its true beginnings even earlier than this in, of all places, the kitchen, where chefs had long since worked out the secret of lightness in cakes and puddings and also the secret of the successful souffle. The principal leavening agent of which was, of course, air. Whether or not the Freres Montgolfier were dedicated gourmets—which seems likely, after all they *were* French—is not known, but their balloon worked on the very same principle which

1

the cooks of France had been applying in their ovens. The expanding hot air which brought towering souffles out of the kitchens of kings sent the Montgolfier balloon soaring into the heavens. Today, we have other means of ascending to the stars, but the souffle—still the crowning glory of many a meal—continues to rely upon expanding heated air to give it the lift which transforms it from a mere leaden mass into an explosion of taste and tenderness.

Just what, then, is a souffle? The word itself derives from the French "souffler," meaning "to breathe, or blow," and there, once again, we find implicit the air upon which successful souffles depend. But in culinary parlance the souffle is anything which, when mixed together, placed in a dish and baked—if done properly—lifts itself by means of expanding air incorporated into beaten egg whites, above and beyond the confines of the dish in which it was originally placed.

The term has also come to mean "anything which in its finished state resembles a souffle" and in this category we find both frozen and gelatin preparations which are made in such a manner that there is more of the mixture than its container will hold. These cold souffles are prepared by tying a removable collar around the top of the small dish to act as a retaining wall until that part of the batter which will not fit into the dish has set or frozen and which, when the supporting device is removed, will stand above the rim of the dish in such a manner as to give the finished item the appearance of having risen on its own from the depths of the container. A trick, to be sure, but a highly effective one which lends charm and grace to dishes which would otherwise appear pedestrain.

To recap slightly—the souffle, then, consists generally of a base which includes fixers and flavors and, in the case of hot baked souffles—without exception—stiffly beaten egg whites! The egg white, when beaten stiffly, breaks down into thousands of tiny balloons, the skins of which contain portions of air. It is the air which, when heated in the oven, expands, stretching the egg-white skin of the balloons, in effect, blowing them up, and through this expansion causes the souffle to rise.

But what of the base? Because the egg whites are of such a delicate nature, the base itself must not be too heavy or the expanding whites will not be able to lift it. Neither must it be too chunky or contain pieces of material too heavy for the whites to lift. The base, usually butter, flour, liquid, egg yolks and flavoring, must not be so stiff as to prevent the easy incorporation of the beaten egg whites, nor, for that matter, can it be too liquid. But like all rules, even these have exceptions. In this volume, we will try to describe the souffles, whose bases are the exceptions to the rule. They will usually be main dish and vegetable souffles.

4

SURE-THING SOUFFLES

The most important thing for you to remember in making a souffle is *don't let it frighten you*. Basically, souffles are simple, and we shall try to explain for you just how to make your souffle take off for the skies in much the same manner as the Montgolfier balloon rose that morning in 1783. Here are some very simple rules to follow on the road to sure-thing souffles.

1. Select a dish of the proper size. No use at all in making the most delicate of souffle batters and then putting it into a dish so large that no matter how high it rises, it cannot reach the top. The souffle will look awful but taste fine. *Rule of thumb: There should be enough souffle batter to fill the dish from 3/4 to 7/8 full.* Then when it starts rising, the only possible place for the souffle to go is *Up*!

2. Do not over-beat the egg whites. If they are too stiff, you will have to work hard to incorporate them into the base and thus break too many of the balloons, lose too much of the air, and hence the lifting power of the whites will be curtailed.

3. Always use one or two more egg whites than yolks, except in some of the vegetable souffles which are not expected to rise as high in the first place. The

extra whites act as lifting insurance and serve to compensate for those balloons which are ruptured during the folding process.

4. *Don't overbake the souffle!* Many books giving recipes for souffles state, in my opinion, cooking times which are far too long. As long as the air in the egg whites keeps expanding, the souffle will continue to rise, until—as in the manner of any balloon—the pressure within becomes too great and the balloon bursts. Many times when we look at our souffle in the oven and find it lying helpless in the bottom of the dish, we are apt to say "Oh dear! The souffle didn't rise!" When actually the chances are that it not only rose, but fell down again when the expanding balloons burst from cooking too long. A good souffle should be

6

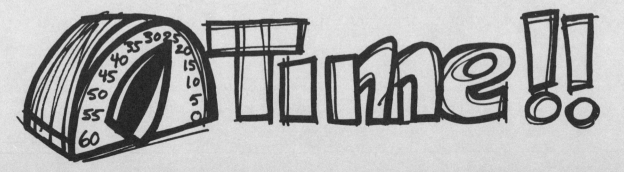

slightly runny and tacky in its center, but well puffed, risen, firm across its top and outer edges and should wobble slightly when skaken gently.

5. Also, you must remember that once in the oven, the cooking time determines the time at which your guests must be prepared to be at the table ready to welcome the souffle hot and high from the oven. The souffle must not, nor will it, wait for your guests. Your guests must await its arrival and to this effect, whenever I plan to serve a souffle for a first course, I lock all the bathroom doors, turn off the cocktails and announce dinner minutes ahead of the time when I expect the souffle to be ready.

So, now, with these few basic rules and the recipes which follow, your souffles should reach for the heavens, although not, we hope, too high as did one I made which rose straight up and stuck to the roof of the oven, and which I had to destroy to get out of the oven. Try and make yours stop 7/16ths of an inch away! Let's get out the eggs and the butter, the souffle dishes, heat the oven, and UP! UP! AND AWAY!!!

A DAINTY DISH

If my memory serves me right, the "dainty dish" consisted of 4 and 20 blackbirds and was served to King Henry VIII. Although the rhyme itself was a political satire of some sort, the term seems applicable to the many types of containers available today, all designed for making and serving souffles.

For without exception, the souffle must be carried directly from the oven to the table and served at once from the dish in which it was cooked. It cannot be transferred to another receptable without endangering its composition, nor should this be attempted under any circumstance. Therefore, the utensil must not only be ovenproof, it must also be attractive enough to grace a table and to this end, manufacturers have designed a myriad of souffle dishes which you will find readily available in almost every type of store. The simplest, and probably the most common, form of souffle holder is made of porcelain with straight sides, a flat bottom and comes in an array of sizes. There are tiny dishes—sometimes called ramekins—holding no more than 1/2 cup of batter which are designed for individual service. And, the range of dishes increases to huge dishes holding many quarts. No matter what their size, these china straight-sided bowls may be used for anything which you wish to cook in the oven and need not be restricted solely to souffles. However, the successful souffle will be easier to create in just such a dish, although you may, if you wish, use any ovenproof container with straight sides. The famous manufacturers of chinaware have almost all come forth with variations of the basic white porcelain souffle dish, embellished with flowers, fruits or vegetables, and in many instances, with dishes for the oven incorporating the same patterns as their table china.

The recipes in this volume will all be for either 4, 6 or 8-cup souffle dishes and I feel that, should you need to create souffles for more people than one dish will serve, it will be better to distribute the batter among several smaller dishes rather than try to create a super-monster souffle, which, if successful will most certainly be impressive, but which chances of failure are far greater than those in smaller vessels. Needless to say, the recipes given here can also be used for creating individual souffles and the only thing to remember is to cut the cooking times given by about 8 minutes.

As yet in this volume, we have not spoken of the versatility of the souffle, which is such that it can be used in just about every portion of the meal with great success. Like the quiche, it is adaptable to every course of the meal, but actually goes the quiche one better by becoming a most effective and gasp-producing dessert when brought toweringly triumphant to the table at the conclusion of the meal.

You will find that the souffle is at home at brunches, luncheons, dinner parties, bridge luncheons or after theatre suppers. It can serve as a main dish, accompanied by a salad, or it can function equally well as a vegetable, a cheese course or as a dessert. You can make a souffle from practically anything handy, as long as you have some butter and eggs about, and it can be an ideal way for using up leftovers. There are so many different souffles that we cannot possibly begin to bring them all to you here, but at least we can try to stimulate your imagination with some souffles which we have liked and which we hope you will like too. Some are simple, some are not, but all of them work on the same principle and should present you with no problems if you follow directions closely.

Certain of the components may be prepared ahead of time, although it will take a bit of last minute preparation. The base of any souffle may be prepared well ahead of time and left at room temperature, providing that a piece of plastic wrap, or other airproof covering is pressed tightly down against its surface to prevent a skin from forming. The egg whites may also be left—it's even better to do so—at room temperature in the bowl in which they will be beaten. Egg whites beat to a greater volume and incorporate more air when beaten at room temperature. However, *under no circumstances may you beat the egg whites ahead*!!!!!!!!!!!

HIGH AND HANDSOME

We've talked a lot about egg whites and we know that no baked souffle is going to be a souffle without them. Proper beating makes the difference. *"Stiff but not dry"—a maddening phrase, but one which appears too frequently in recipes without a proper definition.*

Let's take just a minute and try to come up with a somewhat better explanation. When one commences beating egg whites they first become foamy, then gradually thicken and mount in the bowl until they reach a point at which they cling tightly to the sides of the bowl and do not slip or slide when the bowl is tilted. It is at this precise point, they are considered STIFF, BUT NOT DRY.

Now! If one continues beating the egg whites they will continue for several minutes longer to cling tightly to the bowl, becoming in the process firmer and chunkier until eventually they will let loose of the sides of the bowl and return to their original liquid state. It is at the precise moment just before they let go of the sides after this continued beating, that they may be considered STIFF AND DRY.

And just a bit more about the egg whites—once they pass beyond the STIFF AND DRY state and return to liquid, nothing in the world will induce them to

13

beat stiffly once again.

And still a further word about the type of bowl to be used in beating the whites. Without a doubt, the finest receptacles for beating egg whites are pure copper bowls which are readily available in stores throughout the land. Using a large copper bowl and a very large balloon whip will produce stiffly beaten egg whites of incredible texture—firm, small bubbled, and far and away the best souffle insurance you can procure.

However, I have found that a souffle will be thoroughly successful when the whites are beaten with an electric mixer or even, for that matter, with a hand rotary beater. Bear in mind that the larger the beater, the better the quality of egg whites.

All bowls must be bone dry and contain no extraneous matter. Even one tiny drop of egg yolk will deter the perfect beating of the whites and too much will prevent them from stiffening at all. Under no circumstance should you attempt to beat egg whites either in the blender or in a plastic bowl.

Have fun with these recipes and may all your souffles rise high and handsome.

A BASIC SOUFFLE

(A recipe to study and serve as a guide.)

6 cup well-buttered souffle dish
2 tbs. butter
2 tbs. flour
salt and white pepper

3/4 cup milk
4 egg yolks
6 egg whites

16

Preheat oven to 375°F. Arrange the oven rack to allow ample room above souffle dish. Slightly above center is a good position. Melt butter in saucepan. Remove from heat and stir in flour. Season highly with salt and pepper. Blend milk in gradually, until mixture begins to thicken and assumes the appearance of medium white sauce. *Do not let come to a boil or it will be too thick.* As soon as the sauce begins to thicken, remove from heat. Rapidly beat in egg yolks one at a time. *This is the base of the souffle. At this point it should resemble a medium cream sauce and be thickened but slightly fluid.* Transfer base to a larger bowl. Beat egg whites until they are stiff, but not dry (see page 13). *Fold gently into the base—never the other way around!* Pouring the heavier base onto the stiffly beaten whites would crush the whites. So, although it means one more bowl to wash do it and be sure! When the egg whites have been correctly folded into the base, the finished batter should be thoroughly blended, but retain the consistency of the egg whites and not be runny or fluid. Pour the thoroughly blended batter into prepared souffle dish. It should mount up in the dish and need leveling with a spoon.

Do not jar the souffle dish against the table top to level it as this will force the egg white balloons to burst. Nor should you knock the edge of the spoon or the beaters against the sides of the dish in an attempt to clean them. Striking these utensils sharply against the edge of your hand will produce the same results without the insuing danger to your successful souffle.

Bake souffle in preheated oven 17 minutes. At the end of this time it will have risen clear of the dish, be puffy and browned on top and quite runny in the center. This is the way I prefer my souffles, but for those of you whose tastes differ, and who prefer a souffle to be slightly less runny, the cooking time may be extended to 20 minutes, but no more unless specified.

The cooking time given in this volume will be for the more runny type souffle for, after all, that is the author's privilege. Should you wish, the time of each recipe may be increased by 2 or 3 minutes.

This recipe for Basic Souffle, while it will produce a completely edible—but rather dull tasting souffle—is given here for you to study, rather than emulate—and on the ensuing pages you will find variations and embellishments galore!

SOUFFLES WITH CHEESE

Probably the most versatile of all the souffles are those made from various cheeses. The range of cheeses which can be used is virtually inexhaustible and, depending upon which one you select, the cheese souffle can take its place as a starter, an accompaniment to meat, fish or poultry, be served alone with any number of intriguing salads—other than the ubiquitous rabbit food known as the mixed green salad—or even arrive at table in place of a more traditional dessert.

A perfect light luncheon might, for example, consist of a Sharp Cheddar Cheese Souffle—crusty hot French bread with unsalted butter—peeled and hollowed tomatoes filled with string bean salad—all followed by a bowl of fresh mixed fruits which have been marinated in Kirsch, Grand Marnier or Creme de Menthe.

The same souffle could accompany a fine standing rib roast or lend piquancy to delicately sauteed filets of sole. So, let's move on now and begin with this very practical and delicious addition to your dining pleasure.

CHEDDAR CHEESE SOUFFLE

6 cup, well-buttered souffle dish
2 tbs. butter
2 tbs. flour
3/4 cup milk
salt and cayenne pepper

4 egg yolks
1 cup (4 oz.) grated sharp Cheddar cheese
pinch dry mustard
6 egg whites

20   Preheat oven to 375°F. Melt butter in top of double boiler over direct heat. Remove from heat. Stir in flour. Gradually blend in milk. Season with salt and cayenne pepper. Return to very low heat. Stir constantly until mixture barely begins to thicken and resembles a medium cream sauce. Remove from heat. Continue stirring a moment while sauce thickens a little more. Add egg yolks and cheese alternately. Place over *boiling water*. Stir constantly, to prevent curdling. until cheese is melted. Transfer to a large bowl. Season with mustard. Beat egg whites until stiff, but not dry (see page 13). Thoroughly fold into cheese base. Pour into prepared dish. Bake in preheated oven 17-20 minutes. Serve at once.

ROQUEFORT CHEESE SOUFFLE

Proceed as directed for Cheddar Cheese Souffle but substitute 1 cup of Roquefort cheese which has been forced through a fine strainer. Bake as directed.

GRUYERE CHEESE SOUFFLE

Proceed as directed for Cheddar Cheese Souffle but substitute 4 ounces of grated Gruyere cheese. Bake as directed.

HAM & CHEESE SOUFFLE

Proceed as directed for Cheddar Cheese Souffle, but use only 2 ounces of grated Sharp Cheddar Cheese and 2 ounces of finely ground ham. Bake as directed.

TONGUE & CHEESE SOUFFLE

Proceed as directed for Cheddar Cheese Souffle but substitute 2 ounces of finely grated Cheddar and 2 ounces of finely ground smoked or corned tongue. Bake as directed.

BACON & CHEESE SOUFFLE

Proceed as directed for Cheddar Cheese Souffle but add 3 slices of very crisply fried and finely crumbled bacon. Bake as directed.

PEANUT BUTTER & CHEESE SOUFFLE

Proceed as directed for Cheddar Cheese Souffle but substitute 1/2 cup of peanut butter and only 1/2 cup of finely grated Cheddar cheese. Bake as directed.

TOMATO & CHEESE SOUFFLE

6 cup, well-buttered souffle dish
2 tbs. butter
2 tbs. flour
salt and freshly ground pepper
6 tbs. tomato or V8 juice

6 tbs. milk
4 egg yolks
1 cup (4 oz.) sharp Cheddar cheese
6 egg whites

24   Preheat oven to 375°F. Melt butter in top of double boiler. Remove from heat. Stir in flour. Season to taste with salt and pepper. Gradually stir in juice and milk. Return to heat. Stir constantly until mixture begins to thicken and resembles a medium cream sauce. Remove once again from heat. Continue stirring a moment while sauce thickens a little more. Add egg yolks and cheese alternately. Place pan over boiling water. Stir constantly, to prevent curdling, until cheese has all melted. Transfer to a large bowl. Beat egg whites until stiff, but not dry (see page 13). Fold into cheese base. Pour into prepared dish. Level with spoon. Bake in preheated oven 17-18 minutes or until well risen, puffed and brown. Serve at once.

SOUFFLES WITH VEGETABLES

It seems as if the one category of dishes of which my students cannot get enough is vegetables. American and English tables make a great deal more of the vegetable as an integral part of the meal than do the French. In France the vetetable is so often incorporated into the body of the entree that separate vegetables served with the meal are virtually unknown except for the potato. American diners in French restaurants who order 2 vegetables to accompany their entree often think that the order has been forgotten when the entree appears without them, then are appalled and astounded when, after having glutted themselves on the Filet de Veau Orloff or somesuch, are suddenly confronted with another succeeding course consisting of those very two vegetables which they had ordered and given up for lost.

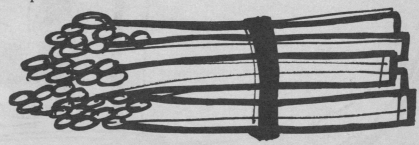

But no thoughtful American hostess would dream of serving her guests anything less than meat, potato and one vegetable, and often, if there is as much as 2 square inches of dinner plate showing, after the food has been portioned upon it, she will fill up this embarrassing bit of china with still another vegetable.

It is in this somewhat vicious search for new and unusual vegetable dishes that the souffle can play a favored role. True! As we have said, the souffle cannot be prepared entirely ahead and this may deter some less adventurous cooks, but with judidious planning and perhaps a five minute wait between courses (not so terrible as one may think—it can give your guests a chance to discover who is setting to either side of them!), you can give an additional filip to your main course and earn the appreciation of friends who will marvel at your being so beautifully organized as to present them with a souffle in the middle of a meal.

Vegetable souffles lend themselves wonderfully to individual service and to my mind there is nothing quite so impressive as being given a little souffle for my very own. It takes no longer than one large souffle, for the time to fill the tiny dishes is regained as the little ones cook for a shorter time.

ARTICHOKE SOUFFLE

4 cup, well-buttered souffle dish
4-1/2 lbs. artichokes
1 lemon
2 cups (10 oz.) potatoes
3 egg yolks

1/2 cup (2 oz.) grated Gruyere cheese
1/4 cup soft butter
salt, freshly ground black pepper
3 egg whites

Preheat oven to 350°F. Cut stems and peel leaves from artichokes. Remove chokes. Rub cut portions with lemon. Cover denuded artichoke hearts with 6 cups boiling water. Add salt, whole peppercorns (not more than 4) and juice of lemon. Cook 25 minutes. Peel and cut potatoes. Place in pot with boiling water to cover. Cook 20 minutes. Drain vegetables. Shake each over heat to dry thoroughly. Put through food mill or other pureeing device. Mix well together. Beat in egg yolks, cheese and butter. Season highly with salt and pepper. Beat egg whites until stiff but not dry (see page 13). Fold carefully into base which is heavier than usual and requires a bit more effort. Pour mixture into prepared dish. Bake in preheated oven 25 minutes or until puffed and nicely browned.

ASPARAGUS SOUFFLE

6 cup, well-buttered souffle dish
1 lb. asparagus
3 tbs. butter
1 small onion, grated
3 tbs. flour

3/4 cup milk
salt and cayenne pepper
4 egg yolks
6 egg whites
Parmesan cheese

Preheat oven to 375°F. Cook enough asparagus tips—fresh or frozen, but not canned—in boiling, salted water to yield 1 cup asparagus puree. Place puree in small saucepan over fairly high heat to drive off excess moisture. In another pan, melt butter. Add onion. Cook until very soft but not brown, Remove from heat. Stir in flour. Gradually pour in milk. Season with salt and cayenne pepper. Return to heat. Stir until sauce begins to thicken. Remove from heat. Add asparagus puree. Beat in egg yolks, one at a time. Correct seasoning to taste. Turn mixture into large bowl. Add egg whites which have been beaten until stiff, but not dry (see page 13). Pour batter into prepared dish. Sprinkle lightly with cheese. Bake in preheated oven 17 minutes. Serve at once.

BEET SOUFFLE I

4 cup, well-buttered souffle dish
1 lb. small beets
1/2 lb. potatoes
3 egg yolks
1/4 cup soft butter
salt and black pepper
3 egg whites

Preheat oven to 350°F. Cook beets in boiling water until tender, at least 25 minutes. Drain and remove skins. Peel potatoes. Cut into chunks. Cook in boiling, salted water 25 minutes. Drain. Return to heat to drive out excess moisture. Force beets and potatoes through food mill or other pureeing device. Transfer to large bowl. Beat in egg yolks and butter. Season highly with salt and pepper. Beat egg whites until stiff, but not dry (see page 13). Fold into beet base. Turn into prepared dish. Bake in preheated oven 25 minutes or until souffle is well-risen, puffed and nicely browned across the top. Serve at once.

BEET SOUFFLE II (BORSCHT SOUFFLE)

6 cup, well-buttered souffle dish
2 tbs. butter
2 tbs. flour
garlic salt, freshly ground black pepper

6 tbs. concentrated beet juice*
6 tbs. sour cream
4 egg yolks
6 egg whites

Preheat oven to 375°F. Melt butter in saucepan. Remove from heat. Stir in flour. Season highly with garlic salt and pepper. Thoroughly blend in beet juice and sour cream. Cook over medium heat until mixture barely begins to thicken. Remove from heat. Beat in egg yolks, one at a time. Transfer base to large bowl. Fold in egg whites which have been beaten until stiff, but not dry (see page 13). Pour batter into prepared dish. Bake in preheated oven 17-20 minutes, or until souffle is well-puffed, set at the edges, brown across the top and wobbles slightly when shaken gently. Serve at once.

*Available at health food stores or diet section of grocery stores.

BROCCOLI SOUFFLE

4 cup, well-buttered souffle dish
1-1/4 lbs. broccoli
1/2 lb. potatoes, peeled and cubed
3 egg yolks
1/2 cup (2 oz.) grated Gruyere cheese
1/4 cup soft butter
3 egg whites

Preheat oven to 350°F. Trim and discard leaves and tough outer covering from stalks of broccoli. Cook in boiling salted water for 15 minutes. In another pot cook potatoes until very soft. Drain both vegetables and return to heat to drive out any excess moisture. Force together through a food mill or other pureeing device. Beat in egg yolks, cheese and butter. Transfer to large bowl. Beat egg whites until stiff, but not dry (see page 13). Fold gently into base. Pour into prepared souffle dish. Bake in preheated oven 25 minutes. Serve immediately.

BRUSSELS SPROUTS SOUFFLE

4 cup, well-buttered (2 tbs.) souffle dish
1-1/4 lbs. small Brussels sprouts
1/2 lb. peeled, cubed potatoes
3 egg yolks

1/2 cup grated Gruyere cheese
1/4 cup soft butter
3 egg whites

34   Preheat oven to 350°F. Remove dark outer leaves from sprouts. Trim away tougher portion of stems. Score bottoms so centers will cook in the same time as leaves. Cook sprouts in boiling, salted water 15 minutes. Cook potatoes until they are very soft. Drain both vegetables. Return to heat to drive out any excess moisture. Force them together through food mill or other pureeing device. Beat in egg yolks, cheese and butter. Transfer to large bowl. Beat egg whites until stiff, but not dry (see page 13). Fold gently into base. Pour into prepared dish. Bake in preheated oven 25 minutes or until souffle has risen well above the lip of the dish and is nicely browned on top. Serve at once.

CAULIFLOWER SOUFFLE

4 cup, well-buttered souffle dish
1-1/4 lbs. cauliflower
1/2 lb. potatoes
3 egg yolks
1/2 cup sour cream

1/4 cup butter
salt, pepper to taste
1 tbs. well-drained horseradish
4 egg whites

Preheat oven to 350°F. Break cauliflower into flowerettes. Cook in boiling salted water 15 minutes. Cook potatoes in another pot until very soft. Drain vegetables. Return to heat to drive out any excess moisture. Force together through food mill or other pureeing device. Beat in egg yolks, sour cream, butter, salt, pepper and horseradish. Transfer base to large bowl. Beat egg whites until stiff, but not dry (see page 13). Fold gently into the base. Pour into prepared dish. Bake in preheated oven 25 minutes or until souffle has puffed, risen well above the lip of the dish and is nicely browned on top. Serve at once.

CARROT SOUFFLE I

Follow the recipe for Broccoli Souffle, substituting 1-1/4 lbs. carrots for the broccoli. Bake as directed.

CARROT SOUFFLE II

Follow the recipe for Beet Souffle II, substituting concentrated carrot juice (available in health food stores or in many markets in the diet foods section) for the beet juice called for. Bake as directed.

CELERY SOUFFLE I

Follow the recipe for Beet Souffle II, substituting concentrated celery juice (available in health food stores or in many markets in the diet foods section) for the beet juice called for. Bake as directed.

CELERY SOUFFLE II

6 cup, well-buttered souffle dish
1 small bunch celery
2 tbs. butter
2 tbs. flour

celery salt, freshly ground black pepper
3/4 cup milk
4 egg yolks
6 egg whites

Preheat oven to 375°F. Remove strings and leaves from celery. Cut into small pieces. Cook in boiling, salted water 25 minutes. Drain well. Force through food mill or other pureeing device. Return puree to a small saucepan. Place over high heat, stirring or shaking to drive out all the excess moisture. Measure 1 cup of this puree. Melt butter in saucepan. Remove from heat. Stir in flour. Season highly with celery salt and pepper. Gradually blend in milk. Cook, stirring constantly, until mixture thickens and resembles medium cream sauce. Remove from heat. Stir a few moments to allow mixture to continue thickening. Cool slightly. Beat in egg yolks and puree. Transfer to large bowl. Beat egg whites until stiff, but not dry (see page 13). Fold into celery base. Pour into prepared dish. Bake in preheated oven 17-20 minutes or until well-puffed and brown.

CELERY ROOT SOUFFLE

6 cup, well-buttered souffle dish
1-3/4 lbs. celery root
1/2 lb. potatoes
1/4 cup soft butter

3/4 cup sour cream
4 egg yolks
6 egg whites
dried bread crumbs

Preheat oven to 350°F. Peel and cut vegetables into chunks. Cook together in boiling salted water 30 minutes. Drain well. Shake pan over heat to drive out excess moisture. Force through food mill or other pureeing device. Add butter and sour cream. Beat in egg yolks. Season highly with salt and freshly ground black pepper. Transfer to large bowl. Beat egg whites until stiff, but not dry (see page 13). Fold into celery root base. Pour mixture into prepared dish. Sprinkle with crumbs. Bake in preheated oven 20-25 minutes or until risen, puffed and nicely browned.

CORN SOUFFLE

6 cup, well-buttered souffle dish
3 ears tender corn
1 tbs. salt
3 tbs. sugar
1/2 cup milk
2 tbs. butter

2 tbs. flour
salt, freshly ground black pepper
1 tbs. Dijon mustard
3/4 cup milk
4 egg yolks
6 egg whites

Preheat oven to 375°F. Fill a pot halfway with water. Add salt, sugar and milk. Bring to boil. Add corn. Boil rapidly for 3-4 minutes. Remove corn. Scrape kernals from cob to measure 1 cup pulp. Melt butter in saucepan. Remove from heat. Stir in flour. Season highly with salt, pepper and mustard. Gradually blend in milk. Stir over medium heat until mixture begins to thicken and resembles medium cream sauce. Remove from heat. Add corn. Beat in egg yolks. Transfer to a large bowl. Beat egg whites until stiff, but not dry (see page 13). Fold into corn base. Pour into prepared souffle dish. Bake in preheated oven 17-20 minutes or until well-puffed and browned on top. Serve immediately.

FENNEL SOUFFLE

Follow directions exactly for Celery Souffle. Substitute 1 bunch fresh fennel for the celery. Bake as directed.

ONION SOUFFLE

6 cup, well-buttered souffle dish
1/2 lb. onions thinly sliced
3 tbs. butter

3 tbs. flour
6 tbs. heavy cream
salt and pepper

4 egg yolks
6 egg whites

Preheat oven to 375°F. Simmer onions and butter in covered pan 30 minutes. Do not brown. Pour into blender. Add flour, cream, salt and pepper. Blend until completely pureed and mixed with flour. Transfer to large bowl. Beat in yolks. Beat egg whites until stiff, but not dry (see page 13). Fold into base. Pour into prepared dish. Bake in preheated oven 17-20 minutes or until well-risen, puffed and nicely browned. Souffle will wobble slightly when shaken gently. Serve at once.

SPINACH SOUFFLE

6 cup, well buttered souffle dish
1 bunch spinach
3 tbs. butter
1 small onion, grated
3 tbs. flour
3/4 cup milk

salt, cayenne pepper
pinch nutmeg
4 egg yolks
7 egg whites
Parmesan cheese

42

Preheat oven to 375°F. Wash and stem spinach. Cook 4-5 minutes using only water clinging to leaves. Drain well. Rinse in cold water. Dry thoroughly and chop coarsely. Melt butter in saucepan. Add onion. Cook, without browning, until very soft. Remove from heat. Stir in flour. Gradually blend in milk. Season. Add spinach. Put in blender until thoroughly mixed. Pour into large bowl. Beat in egg yolks. Beat whites until stiff, but not dry (see page 13). Gently fold into spinach base. Pour into prepared dish. Sprinkle lightly with cheese. Bake 17-20 minutes or until well-risen, puffed and nicely browned. Serve immediately.

TOMATO SOUFFLE

6 cup, well-buttered souffle dish
1 lb. ripe tomatoes
3 tbs. butter
1/2 chicken bouillon cube
1 tsp. tomato paste
pinch sugar

3 tbs. flour
3/4 cup milk
salt, freshly ground pepper
4 egg yolks
6 egg whites

Preheat oven to 375°F. Peel and seed tomatoes. Chop very, very fine. Melt butter in frying pan. Add tomatoes and bouillon. Cook until juices have been cooked away entirely. Stir in tomato paste and sugar. Remove from heat. Blend in flour. Stir in milk. Cook over medium heat until mixture barely begins to thicken. Season highly with salt and pepper. Remove from heat and beat in yolks, one at a time. Transfer to large bowl. Beat whites until stiff, but not dry (see page 13). Fold carefully into base. Pour into prepared dish. Bake in preheated oven 17-20 minutes, or until well-risen and browned on top. Serve at once.

AVOCADO SOUFFLE

6 cup, well-buttered souffle dish
2-3 very ripe avocados
salt, freshly ground black pepper
1 tsp. lemon juice
1 tbs. mayonnaise

2 tbs. butter
2 tbs. flour
3/4 cup buttermilk
4 egg yolks
6 egg whites

44   Preheat oven to 375°F. Peel and pit enough avocados to yield 1 cup pulp when passed through a fine sieve. Season highly with salt and pepper. Sprinkle with lemon juice. Beat in mayonnaise. Melt butter in saucepan. Remove from heat. Blend in flour. Gradually add buttermilk. Season to taste. Stir over moderate heat until mixture barely begins to thicken. Remove from heat. Continue stirring for a moment. Beat in yolks, one at a time. Add avocado puree. Transfer to a large bowl. Beat whites until stiff but not dry (see page 13). Fold into base. Pour into prepared dish. Bake in preheated oven 17-20 minutes, or until the souffle is well-risen, puffed and browned across the top. Serve at once.

POTATO SOUFFLE

6 cup, well-buttered souffle dish
1 lb. potatoes
1/4 cup butter
1/2 cup (2 oz.) grated Gruyere cheese

1/2 cup cream
salt, white pepper
4 egg yolks
6 egg whites

Preheat oven to 375°F. Peel potatoes, preferably not Idahos. Cut into chunks. Boil in salted water for 15 minutes. Drain. Return to heat, shaking rapidly to drive off excess moisture. (Potatoes will appear floury). Force through food mill or other pureeing device. Beat in butter, cheese and cream. Season with salt and pepper. Beat in egg yolks. Transfer mixture to large bowl. Beat egg whites until stiff, but not dry (see page 13). Gently fold into base. Pour into prepared dish. Bake in preheated oven 17-20 minutes or until souffle has risen well above the lip of the dish, is puffy and browned on top. It will wobble slightly when shaken gently. Serve at once.

ORANGE SWEET POTATO SOUFFLE

6 cup, well-buttered souffle dish
1 lb. yams or sweet potatoes
1/4 cup butter
1/2 cup milk

3/4 cup Grand Marnier*
salt, pepper, pinch nutmeg
4 egg yolks
6 egg whites

Preheat oven to 375°F. Peel sweet potatoes. Cut in chunks. Boil in salted water 15 minutes. Drain well. Return to heat, shaking briskly to drive out any excess moisture. (Potatoes will appear floury). Force through food mill or other pureeing device. Beat in butter, milk and Grand Marnier. Season highly with salt, pepper, and nutmeg. Beat in egg yolks. Transfer to large bowl. Beat whites until stiff, but not dry (see page 13). Fold gently into base. Pour into prepared dish. Bake in preheated oven until souffle has risen, appears well-puffed and is browned across the top. It will wobble slightly when shaken gently. Serve immediately.

*or other orange flavored liqueur.

SAUERKRAUT SOUFFLE

6 cup, well-buttered souffle dish
1 lb. sauerkraut
3 tbs. butter
3 tbs. flour
3/4 cup milk

salt and pepper
4 egg yolks
1 tbs. caraway seeds
6 egg whites

Preheat oven to 375°F. Cook sauerkraut in its own juice until very tender. Drain and squeeze kraut completely dry. Melt butter in saucepan. Add sauerkraut. Cook 20 minutes over very low heat. Do not brown. Remove from heat. Add flour, milk and seasonings. Return to heat. Cook only until mixture begins to barely thicken. Put in blender on highest speed until pureed. Pour into large bowl. Beat in egg yolks. Stir in caraway seeds. Beat egg whites until stiff, but not dry (see page 13). Fold into base, gently but thoroughly. Spoon into prepared dish. Bake in preheated oven 17-20 minutes or until souffle has risen high and is nicely browned across the top. Serve immediately.

MUSHROOM SOUFFLE

6 cup, well-buttered souffle dish
1/2 lb. mushrooms
3 tbs. butter
1 finely minced shallot
2 tbs. flour

3/4 cup milk
salt, cayenne pepper
4 egg yolks
6 egg whites

Preheat oven to 375°F. Remove stems from mushrooms. Mince caps very finely. Melt 1 tablespoon butter in saucepan. Add shallot. Cook slowly until soft. *Do not let brown*. Add mushrooms. Cook until dry. Keep heat low and cook slowly. Melt 2 tablespoons butter in top of glass or enamaled double boiler over direct heat. Remove from heat. Stir in flour. Blend in milk. Add salt and cayenne to taste. Return pot to very low heat. Stir constantly until sauce just begins to thicken. Remove from heat. Continue stirring to thicken slightly. Beat in egg yolks, one at a time. Place over boiling water. Add mushrooms. Stir briskly a few moments until sauce thickens a bit more. Remove immediately. Pour into large bowl. Beat egg whites until stiff, but not dry (see page 13). Fold carefully into base. Pour into prepared dish. Bake in preheated oven 17-20 minutes or until souffle has risen well above the lip of the dish, is puffy, brown and wobbles slightly when shaken gently. Serve at once.

MAIN COURSE SOUFFLES

Although the souffle and the quiche differ in appearance and taste, makeup and texture, the uses to which they may both be put are very similar. Both dishes lend themselves most admirably to service in almost any part of the meal and can be made from almost anything. But the souffle seems perhaps more at home as an accompaniment dish or as a principal dish for either a luncheon or brunch than for dinner.

However, there are many souffles which utilize fish and poultry and these can be pressed into service as main courses when preceded by a hearty meal-opener, such as thick soup, or a molded salad, or, perhaps, a stuffed tomato or avocado. As we have said in an earlier chapter, the timing may be a bit trickier, but should not cause too great a problem if the simple suggestions offered earlier are adhered to. Plan a menu that is easy to handle, otherwise, and let the souffle be the only item requiring last minute attention. Make the base ahead and cover with plastic wrap to prevent it from drying on top. Place the egg whites in the bowl in which they are to be beaten and allow to stand at room temperature. They will beat much better, but please, don't put the whip to them until it's time to finish the souffle.

CHICKEN SOUFFLE I

CREAMED CHICKEN

1 whole chicken breast
1 onion, sliced
1 carrot, sliced
2 stalks celery, sliced
bay leaf, salt, pepper

2 cups milk
2 tbs. butter
3 tbs. flour
salt, cayenne pepper

1 tsp. Dijon mustard
2 egg yolks
1/2 cup whipping cream
6 cup, well-buttered souffle dish

52

Split breast in half. Leave skin on. Place in shallow pan with onion, carrot, celery, bay leaf, salt and pepper. Add milk. Bring slowly to boil. Simmer until chicken is done, about 10 minutes on each side. Remove chicken. Cool. Strain and save milk. *Measure 3/4 cup. Set aside for use in souffle later.* Melt butter in saucepan. Remove from heat. Stir in flour. Season to taste with salt and cayenne. Add mustard. Blend in 1 cup strained milk. Return to heat. Stir until sauce boils. Remove from heat. Beat egg yolks into cream. Add to hot sauce. Cut chicken into cubes. Add to sauce. Pour into souffle dish. Set aside.

SOUFFLE

2 tbs. butter
2 tbs. flour
salt, cayenne pepper
3/4 cup reserved milk
4 egg yolks
6 egg whites

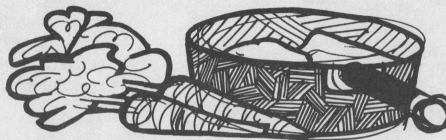

53

Preheat oven to 375°F. Melt butter in saucepan. Remove from heat. Add flour and season to taste. Blend in milk. Return to heat. Stir constantly until sauce just begins to thicken. Remove from heat. Beat in egg yolks. Beat whites until stiff, but not dry (see page 13). Fold into base. Pour over Creamed Chicken. Bake in preheated oven 17-20 minutes. Serve at once.

CHICKEN SOUFFLE II

6 cup, well-buttered souffle dish
2 lbs. chicken breasts
3 tsp. butter
2 tsp. flour
salt, cayenne pepper
1/2 tsp. dry mustard
1/3 cup milk

2 tbs. sherry
3 egg yolks
1/4 tsp. nutmeg
1/2 tsp. anchovy paste
1 cup cream, whipped
5 egg whites

Preheat oven to 375°F. Put raw chicken through finest blade of meat grinder, twice. Then force through food mill or other pureeing device. Melt butter in saucepan. Remove from heat. Stir in flour. Season with salt, cayenne and mustard. Blend in milk. Return to heat. Stir constantly until sauce boils. Remove from heat. Add sherry. Beat in egg yolks and pureed chicken. Pour into large bowl. Season with nutmeg and anchovy paste. Blend in whipped cream. Beat whites until stiff, but not dry (see page 13). Fold into base. Pour into prepared dish. Bake in preheated oven 25-30 minutes. *This makes a heavier souffle than usual.*

TURKEY SOUFFLE

4 cup, well-buttered souffle dish
1 lb. cooked turkey
4 egg yolks

salt, pinch nutmeg, poultry seasoning
3/4 cup cream, whipped
6 egg whites

Preheat oven to 375°F. Put turkey through grinder twice, using finest blade. Beat egg yolks into ground meat. Season highly with salt, nutmeg and poultry seasoning. Force mixture through food mill or other pureeing device. Blend whipped cream into pureed meat. Beat egg whites until stiff, but not dry (see page 13). Fold into turkey base. Pour into prepared dish. Bake in preheated oven 20-25 minutes, or until well-risen and brown. Serve at once.

SMOKED TURKEY SOUFFLE

Follow directions for Turkey Souffle. Substitute smoked turkey and eliminate poultry seasoning. Bake as directed.

FINAN HADDIE SOUFFLE

6 cup, well-buttered souffle dish
1/2 lb. finan haddie
3 tbs. butter
1 chopped shallot
salt and white pepper

3 tbs. flour
1 cup milk
4 egg yolks
6 egg whites

Soak finan haddie several hours in cold water. Change water twice during the soaking period. Drain. Place fish in saucepan. Add 1 tablespoon butter, shallot, salt and pepper. Barely cover fish with water. Bring to boil, cover pan, and simmer about 20 minutes or until fish is thoroughly done. Drain well. Force through food mill or other pureeing device. Preheat oven to 375°F. In another saucepan melt remaining butter. Remove from heat. Add flour. Gradually blend in milk. Return to heat. Stir constantly until sauce·begins to thicken. Remove from heat. Add fish. Mix well. Taste for seasoning. Beat in egg yolks. Transfer to large bowl. Beat egg whites until stiff, but not dry (see page 13). Fold into base. Pour into prepared dish. Bake in preheated oven 20-25 minutes. Serve immediately.

SALMON SOUFFLE I

6 cup, well buttered souffle dish
1-3/4 lbs. raw salmon
3 tsp. butter
2 tsp. flour
1/2 tsp. mustard
1 tsp. dill weed
salt, cayenne pepper

1/3 cup milk
3 egg yolks
2 tsp. Sherry or Madeira
nutmeg, anchovy paste
1 cup cream, whipped
5 egg whites

Preheat oven to 375°F. Put salmon through finest blade of meat grinder, twice. Then force through food mill or other pureeing device. Melt butter in saucepan. Remove from heat. Stir in flour, mustard and dill weed. Season to taste. Blend in milk. Stir constantly over medium heat until mixture boils. Remove from heat. Beat in egg yolks and and wine. Add salmon. Season with nutmeg and anchovy paste to taste. Fold in cream. Beat egg whites until stiff, but not dry (see page 13). Carefully fold into base. Pour into prepared dish. Bake in preheated oven 20-25 minutes or until well-risen and set. This souffle is similar in type and texture to Chicken Souffle II.

SALMON SOUFFLE HOLLANDAISE

This glorious dish is only partly a souffle, but so grand an affair that it would be almost criminal not to include it. Complicated to be sure, but worth the time spent preparing it. Your guests will bless you for your noble efforts.

STEP I

1 lb. fresh spinach, washed	3/4 cup white wine	1 sliced onion
1 tbs. butter	salt, peppercorns	1 sliced carrot
4 lb. piece fresh salmon	bay leaf, thyme, parsley	2 stalks celery

Chop spinach very fine. Cook in butter, seasoned with salt, pepper and dash of lemon juice, until vegetable juices have been cooked away. Set aside for later use. Cut 6 fillets from salmon piece. Put in shallow baking dish. Place remaining skin and bones in saucepan with other ingredients. Simmer gently 20 minutes. Strain broth over fillets. Cover with waxed paper. Poach in 250°F. oven 15 minutes. Strain off liquid into saucepan. Keep fillets warm, covered, in *very low* oven. Reduce liquid to 1/3 its original amount for use in Souffle Base on page 60.

SOUFFLE BASE

1 tbs. butter

1 tbs. flour

salt, cayenne pepper

6 tbs. reduced fish broth

2 egg yolks

60   Melt butter in saucepan. Remove from heat. Stir in flour and seasonings. Blend in fish broth. Return to heat. Stir constantly until it barely begins to thicken. Remove from heat. Beat in egg yolks. Cover with plastic. Set aside until needed.

HOLLANDAISE SAUCE

2 egg yolks   juice 1/2 lemon   1/4 lb. butter
2 tbs. cream   salt, cayenne pepper

Combine ingredients in saucepan. Stir over very low heat until mixture thickens and becomes a soft custard. Remove from heat. Continue stirring for a few moments to prevent sauce from curdling in its own heat.

61

FINAL STEP

3 egg whites

Preheat oven to 425°F. Arrange poached salmon on lightly buttered, flameproof dish. Spread each fillet with prepared spinach. Beat egg whites until stiff, but not dry (see page 13). Fold into Souffle Base. Mask salmon with souffle mixture. Spread Hollandaise gently and carefully over souffle. Bake in preheated oven 10 minutes or until puffed and nicely browned. Serve immediately.

SMOKED SALMON & DILL SOUFFLE

6 cup, well-buttered souffle dish
1 cup (6-8 oz.) smoked salmon
2 tbs. butter
2 tbs. flour
salt, freshly ground pepper

1 tbs. dried dill weed
3/4 buttermilk
4 egg yolks
6 egg whites

62   Preheat oven to 375°F. Put salmon through the fine blade of meat grinder. Then force through a food mill or other pureeing device. Melt butter in saucepan. Remove from heat. Stir in flour. Season with salt, pepper and dill weed. Gradually add buttermilk. Cook over moderate heat until sauce barely begins to thicken. Remove from heat. Stir in salmon. Beat in egg yolks, one at a time. Transfer to large bowl. Beat egg whites until stiff, but not dry (see page 13). Spoon mixture into prepared dish. Bake in preheated oven 17-20 minutes.

LOBSTER SOUFFLE

6 cup, well-buttered souffle dish
1 live lobster or
2-2-1/2 lbs. lobster tails
2 stalks celery
2 onions
2 carrots
6 tbs. butter
1/3 cup brandy

1 cup white wine
1/2 cup heavy cream
salt, pepper, paprika
2 tbs. butter
2 tbs. flour
3/4 cup milk
4 egg yolks
6 egg whites

Preheat oven to 375°F. Remove eyes, the sac behind them and the intestine from live lobster. Chop celery, onions and carrots fine. Melt butter in kettle. Stir in vegetables. Add lobster, still in shell. Saute briskly until bright red. Pour brandy over and ignite. When flame goes out, add wine. Simmer gently 15 minutes. Take lobster from pot. When cool enough to handle, remove meat from body and claws. Place meat in prepared souffle dish. Add cream to liquid in kettle. Cook down until it thickens. Add extra butter if necessary for a nice consistency. Strain out vegetables and adjust seasonings. Pour half over lobster meat. Serve the rest with the souffle. Melt butter in saucepan. Remove from heat. Add flour and seasonings. Gradually blend in milk. Return to low heat. Stir until sauce begins to thicken. Remove from heat. Beat in yolks one at a time. Beat egg whites until stiff, but not dry (see page 13). Carefully fold into base. Pour over lobster. Bake in preheated oven 17-20 minutes or until puffy and brown. Serve with sauce.

LOBSTER SOUFFLE POMPADOUR

6 cup, well-buttered souffle dish
1 live lobster
2 tbs. oil
1/2 cup dry white wine
1/4 cup butter
3 fresh mushrooms
1 fresh tomato

1/2 tsp. tomato paste
pinch sugar
3 tbs. flour
2 tbs. Parmesan cheese
3/4 cup milk
4 egg yolks
6 egg whites

Preheat oven to 375°F. Split lobster in half. Remove eyes, the sac behind and intestines. Remove coral, if any, and liver. Heat oil in deep pot. Place lobster halves in pot, cut side down. Cover and cook quickly until lobster turns red. Add wine. Reduce heat. Cover and cook for 5 minutes. Remove lobster. Add coral and liver. Continue cooking 2 minutes. Pour off liquid and reserve. Remove meat from lobster. Chop coarsely. Melt 2 tablespoons butter in saucepan. When very hot add thinly sliced mushrooms. Brown quickly. Add peeled, seeded and chopped tomato. Reduce it to puree. Remove from heat. Add tomato paste, sugar and 1 tablespoon flour. Stir in reserved lobster liquid. Season with salt and cayenne. Return to heat. Stir until mixture boils. Add Parmesan and lobster. Place on bottom of prepared souffle dish. Melt remaining butter in saucepan. Remove from heat. Add 2 tablespoons flour. Season to taste with salt and cayenne. Blend in milk. Stir constantly over low heat until sauce barely begins to thicken. Remove from heat. Beat in yolks. Fold in egg whites which have been beaten until stiff, but not dry (see page 13). Pour mixture over lobster. Bake in preheated oven 17-20 minutes, or until well-risen, puffy and brown. Serve immediately.

LOBSTER SOUFFLE THERMIDOR

6 cup, well-buttered souffle dish
5 tbs. melted butter
1 live lobster
salt and pepper
1 medium onion
1/2 cup dry white wine
2 tbs. flour

3/4 cup milk
1/4 cup cream
pinch dry mustard, paprika
2 tbs. Parmesan cheese
4 egg yolks
6 egg whites

Preheat oven to 375°F. Place lobster in kettle with cold water to cover. Bring to boil over moderate heat. Simmer gently 5 minutes. Drain. Immediately cover lobster with cold water to prevent further cooking. Split lobster in half. Remove meat from body and claws. Cut in small pieces. Toss with 2 tablespoons melted butter. Arrange in bottom of prepared dish. Chop onion very fine. Saute in frying pan with 2 tablespoons butter until translucent. Do not allow to brown. Add wine. Cook until wine evaporates. Combine flour with remaining butter in saucepan. Add salt and cayenne. Blend in milk. Stir over medium heat until sauce boils. Add onions. Stir in cream, seasonings and cheese. Beat in egg yolks. Transfer mixture to larger bowl. Beat egg whites until stiff, but not dry (see page 13). Fold carefully into base. Pour over lobster. Bake in preheated oven 17-20 minutes or until well-risen, puffy and nicely browned on top. Serve immediately.

CRAB SOUFFLE NEWBERG

Follow the recipe for Lobster Souffle Thermidor. Substitute 1/2 pound crabmeat for the lobster meat. Use a medium dry sherry instead of white wine. Bake as directed.

TUNA SOUFFLE

6 cup, well-buttered souffle dish   4 egg yolks
1 can (7 oz.) tuna   6 egg whites
2 tbs. finely minced celery
2 tbs. grated onion
salt, pepper, Dijon mustard
1/2 lb. peeled potatoes
3 tbs. soft butter
6 tbs. cream

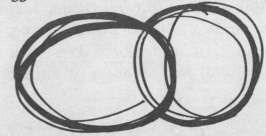

Preheat oven to 375°F. Force tuna through food mill. Mix with celery, onion and seasonings to taste. Cook potatoes in boiling salted water for 20 minutes. Drain. Return to heat to drive out any excess moisture. Force through food mill. Beat in butter and cream. Add tuna. Beat in egg yolks one at a time. Transfer to a large bowl. Beat egg whites until stiff, but not dry (see page 13). Pour into prepared dish. Bake in preheated oven 17-20 minutes or until risen above the lip of the dish, well browned and puffy. Serve at once.

OYSTER AND SPINACH SOUFFLE

6 cup, well-buttered souffle dish
1 tbs. butter
3 peeled carrots
salt, cayenne pepper
1/2 tsp. sugar
1/4 cup water
1 small bunch spinach

4 tsp. flour
1/4 cup chicken broth
1/2 cup milk
1 tbs. Japanese Oyster Sauce
4 egg yolks
6 egg whites

Preheat oven to 375°F. Melt butter in saucepan. Stir in sliced carrots, salt, cayenne, sugar and water. Cover. Cook slowly 5 minutes. Add washed and stemmed spinach. Continue cooking until carrots are very soft. Remove from heat. Thoroughly blend in flour. Add broth and milk. Return to heat. Stir constantly until mixture boils. Puree in blender. Pour into large bowl. Add oyster sauce. Beat in egg yolks. Beat egg whites until stiff, but not dry (see page 13). Pour into prepared dish. Bake in preheated oven 17-20 minutes or until well-risen, puffed and brown on top. Serve at once.

DESSERT SOUFFLE

And now the souffle truly comes into its own. For it is as a dessert that I, at any rate, find the souffle most impressive. A beautiful towering souffle can raise to heights of glory what, up to that point, has been a humdrum meal and send your guests away from the table praising your culinary abilities to the skies.

But, once again, you are going to have to spend a few moments in the kitchen beating the egg whites, folding them in, and putting the dish in the oven. I do this before I begin clearing away the preceding course. Then, when the table has been changed, the dessert plates put down, and the coffee served, there is hardly any time left at all before the souffle is done.

Never do I start the souffle and then worry all through the meal that some slow eater is going to feel rushed because the souffle is done and ready to come to the table.

Dessert souffles require no more doing than the ones in the preceding chapters, but almost without exception (chocolate being that one which disproves the rule!) dessert souffles require a band of buttered waxed paper tied around the dish extending above the rim to prevent the souffle from spilling before it has a chance to set. This is done because the batter for dessert souffles is generally lighter in texture than the other, therefore it rises more quickly and yet takes slightly longer to cook until set enough to hold. You may notice a small amount of smoke and a faint smell of wax during the cooking time but neither is detrimental to the souffle, nor dangerous.

I find that dessert souffles generally do better in an 8 cup souffle dish and I personally prefer to sugar the buttered dish to provide a nice chewy crust to my souffles. There are, in fact, many different schools of thought about buttering souffle dishes. There are those who feel buttering the dish makes it easier for the souffle to rise and there are those others who feel that the sides of the dish must be dry in order to give the souffle something to grab as it climbs up out of the dish, much in the manner of a man trying to find a toehold after falling down a well. To my mind, both of these theories are arrant nonsense, since we have demonstrated earlier in this volumn that expanding air properly incorporated into the beaten egg whites is the sole lifting agent. Butter or don't butter, as you wish; but to my way of thinking, buttering is preferable because the crust will then be available for eating. *Do not, however, sugar the waxed paper band*. Butter the dish, sugar it, butter the paper separately, and *then* tie the *buttered paper* about the outside of the dish in such a way that the string will be easy to remove without disturbing the souffle too much.

Once again, there are so many, many dessert souffles that it would require a separate book to list them all and then most probably there would be still more the very next day. So here, then, are a few of the more delicious ones designed to stimulate your taste buds and your imagination.

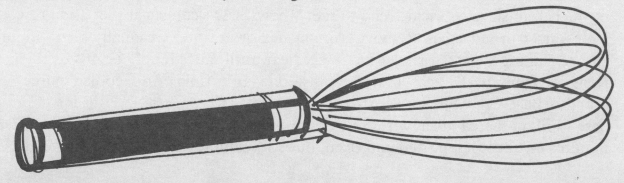

APRICOT SOUFFLE

6 cup, well-buttered souffle dish
1-1/2 cups cooked, dried apricots
1/2 cup sugar
3 tbs. butter
3 tbs. flour

3/4 cup milk
4 egg yolks
2 tbs. apricot brandy
7 egg whites

Preheat oven to 375°F. Sprinkle buttered souffle dish with a little sugar. Tie band of buttered waxed paper around top of dish to extend sides. Force apricots through fine sieve to yield 1 cup puree. Mix with 1/4 cup sugar. Set aside to cool. Melt butter in saucepan. Remove from heat. Stir in flour. Gradually blend in milk and remaining sugar. Stir over moderate heat until sauce barely begins to thicken. Remove from heat. Beat in egg yolks, one at a time. Add cooled puree and brandy. Beat egg whites until stiff, but not dry (see page 13). Fold into apricot base. Fill prepared dish with souffle mixture. Bake in preheated oven 17-20 minutes or until well-puffed and risen, but still wobbles when lightly shaken.

BANANA SOUFFLE

4 cup, well-buttered souffle dish
2 tbs. butter
2 tbs. flour
2 tbs. sugar
1-1/2 cups milk

6 bananas
1 - 2 tbs. Creme de Banan or rum
3 egg yolks
5 egg whites
2 teaspoons sugar

Preheat oven to 375°F. Sprinkle dish with a little sugar. Tie band of buttered waxed paper around top of dish to extend sides. Melt butter in saucepan. Remove from heat. Add flour and sugar. Gradually blend in milk. Return to heat. Stir until mixture boils. Peel bananas. Put through food mill or other pureeing device. Add to sauce. Stir in flavoring. Beat in egg yolks one at a time. Transfer to large bowl. Beat egg whites until stiff, but not dry (see page 13). Add 2 teaspoons sugar. Beat 30 seconds longer. Fold into banana base. Pour into prepared dish. Bake in preheated oven 20-22 minutes. Remove from oven and carefully loosen collar. Sift confectioner's sugar over top. Serve at once.

CHOCOLATE SOUFFLE

6 cup, well-buttered souffle dish
3/4 cup milk
2 ozs. bitter chocolate
7 tbs. sugar

3 tbs. butter
3 tbs. flour
5 egg yolks
7 egg whites

Preheat oven to 375°F. Sprinkle inside of buttered souffle dish with a little sugar. Heat milk, chocolate and 2 tablespoons sugar together in a small saucepan until chocolate is melted. Set aside. Melt butter in a medium-size saucepan. Remove from heat. Stir in flour and 4 tablespoons sugar. Gradually stir in chocolate-milk-sugar mixture. Return to heat. Stir until mixture thickens and resembles a chocolate cream sauce. Remove from heat. Very rapidly beat egg yolks into chocolate mixture. Transfer to a large bowl. Beat egg whites until stiff, but not dry (see page 13.) Add the remaining tablespoon of sugar. Beat 30 seconds. Fold into chocolate base. Pour into prepared souffle dish. Bake in preheated oven 20 minutes. Serve at once.

COFFEE SOUFFLE

8 cup, well-buttered souffle dish
3 tbs. butter
2 tbs. flour
1 tbs. instant coffee
3/4 cup hot milk

5 egg yolks
2 tbs. sugar
6 tbs. Kahlua
6 egg whites
2 tsp. sugar

80   Preheat oven to 375°F. Sprinkle dish with a little sugar. Tie band of buttered, waxed paper around top of dish to extend sides. Melt butter in saucepan. Remove from heat. Stir in flour. Return to heat. Continue cooking until mixture bubbles slightly. Remove from heat. Dissolve coffee in hot milk. Stir into butter-flour mixture. Return to heat. Stir until sauce becomes very thick and boils. Start timing and stir for 5 minutes. Remove from heat. Combine egg yolks and sugar. Quickly beat into sauce. Add Kahlua (or other coffee flavored liqueur). Transfer to large bowl. Beat egg whites until stiff, but not dry (see page 13). Add 2 teaspoons sugar. Beat 30 seconds. Fold into coffee base. Pour into prepared dish. Bake in preheated oven 20-22 minutes or until well-risen. Serve immediately.

DATE SOUFFLE

6 cup, well-buttered souffle dish
1 cup sliced dates
1/2 cup sherry
3 tbs. butter
3 tbs. flour

5 tbs. sugar
3/4 cup milk
5 egg yolks
7 egg whites

Preheat oven to 375°F. Sprinkle dish with a little sugar. Tie a collar of buttered waxed paper around rim of dish to extend sides. Soak dates in sherry until they are very soft. Force through food mill or other pureeing device. Melt butter in saucepan. Remove from heat. Stir in flour and 4 tablespoons sugar. Gradually blend in milk. Return to heat. Stir until mixture barely begins to thicken. Remove from heat. Stir in date puree. Beat in egg yolks. Transfer to large bowl. Beat egg whites until stiff, but not dry (see page 13). Add 1 tablespoon sugar. Beat 30 seconds. Fold into date base. Pour into prepared dish. Bake in preheated oven 20-22 minutes or until well-risen, puffed and brown. Sieve confectioner's sugar over top. Serve at once.

LEMON SOUFFLE

Follow directions for Chocolate Souffle. Omit chocolate and add the grated rind of 1 lemon and 1 to 2 tablespoons lemon juice to sauce after it has been removed from heat. Tie a buttered, waxed paper collar around top of well-buttered souffle dis to extend the sides. Bake as directed.

ORANGE SOUFFLE

Follow directions for Chocolate Souffle. Omit chocolate and add the grated rind of 1 small orange and 2 tablespoons orange juice to sauce after it has been removed from heat. For a stronger flavor, add 2 tablespoons defrosted orange juice concentrate. Tie a buttered waxed paper collar around top of buttered dish to extend sides. Bake as directed.

PRUNE SOUFFLE

Follow directions for Chocolate Souffle. Omit chocolate. Add 1 jar strained prunes and 2 tablespoons Slivovitz or other prune or plum flavored liqueur. Tie a buttered, waxed paper collar around top of buttered dish to extend sides. Bake as directed.

84

LIQUEUR SOUFFLE

8 cup, well-buttered souffle dish

3 tbs. butter

2 tbs. flour

3/4 cup hot milk

5 egg yolks

2 tbs. sugar

6 tbs. liqueur

6 egg whites

Preheat oven to 375° F. Sprinkle dish with a little sugar. Tie a collar of buttered waxed paper around rim of dish. Melt butter in saucepan. Remove from heat. Blend in flour. Return to heat. Cook until mixture bubbles slightly. Remove again. Blend in hot milk. Stir over medium heat until sauce becomes very thick and boils. Start timing and stir five minutes. Remove from heat. Combine egg yolks with 2 tablespoons sugar. Rapidly beat into sauce. Add your favorite liqueur or a combination of liqueurs. Transfer to large bowl. Beat egg whites until stiff, but not dry (see page 13). Add 2 teaspoons sugar. Beat 30 seconds. Fold into liqueur base. Pour into prepared dish. Bake in preheated oven 20-22 minutes. Remove collar and serve immediately.

STRAWBERRY SOUFFLE

8 cup, well-buttered souffle dish
3 tbs. butter
2 tbs. flour
1/2 cup hot milk
5 egg yolks

1/4 cup sugar
1 cup fresh strawberries
1-2 tbs. liqueur or brandy
6 egg whites
2 tsp. sugar

Preheat oven to 375° F. Sprinkle buttered souffle dish with a little sugar. Tie collar of buttered, waxed paper around rim of dish to extend sides. Melt butter in saucepan. Remove from heat. Blend in flour. Return to heat. Stir until mixture begins to turn golden. Add milk. Cook, stirring constantly, 3 to 5 minutes. Take pan from heat. Combine egg yolks with 2 tablespoons sugar. Quickly beat into sauce mixture. Chop strawberries very, very fine. Blend in 2 tablespoons sugar and liqueur. Add to egg mixture. Transfer to large bowl. Beat egg whites until stiff, but not dry (see page 13). Add 2 teaspoons sugar. Beat 30 seconds. Fold carefully into strawberry base. Pour into prepared dish. Bake in preheated oven 20-25 minutes or until well-risen. Sieve confectioner's sugar over top. Serve at once.

INDEX

METRIC CONVERSION CHART

**Liquid or Dry Measuring
Cup (based on an 8 ounce cup)**

1/4 cup = 60 ml
1/3 cup = 80 ml
1/2 cup = 125 ml
3/4 cup = 190 ml
1 cup = 250 ml
2 cups = 500 ml

**Liquid or Dry Measuring
Cup (based on a 10 ounce cup)**

1/4 cup = 80 ml
1/3 cup = 100 ml
1/2 cup = 150 ml
3/4 cup = 230 ml
1 cup = 300 ml
2 cups = 600 ml

**Liquid or Dry
Teaspoon and Tablespoon**

1/4 tsp. = 1.5 ml
1/2 tsp. = 3 ml
1 tsp. = 5 ml
3 tsp. = 1 tbs. = 15 ml

Temperatures

°F		°C
200	=	100
250	=	120
275	=	140
300	=	150
325	=	160
350	=	180
375	=	190
400	=	200
425	=	220
450	=	230
475	=	240
500	=	260
550	=	280

Pan Sizes (1 inch = 25 mm)

8-inch pan (round or square) = 200 mm x 200 mm
9-inch pan (round or square) = 225 mm x 225 mm
9 x 5 x 3-inch loaf pan = 225 mm x 125 mm x 75 mm
1/4 inch thickness = 5 mm
1/8 inch thickness = 2.5 mm

Pressure Cooker

100 Kpa = 15 pounds per square inch
70 Kpa = 10 pounds per square inch
35 Kpa = 5 pounds per square inch

Mass

1 ounce = 30 g
4 ounces = 1/4 pound = 125 g
8 ounces = 1/2 pound = 250 g
16 ounces = 1 pound = 500 g
2 pounds = 1 kg

Key (America uses an 8 ounce cup - Britain uses a 10 ounce cup)

ml = milliliter
l = liter
g = gram
K = Kilo (one thousand)
mm = millimeter
m = milli (a thousandth)
°F = degrees Fahrenheit

°C = degrees Celsius
tsp. = teaspoon
tbs. = tablespoon
Kpa = (pounds pressure per square inch)
This configuration is used for pressure
cookers only.

Metric equivalents are rounded to conform to existing metric measuring utensils.